BORN TO REIGN

BORN TO REIGN

Reno I. Johnson

Fresh Touch Publishing
www.arjm.org
P. O. Box 162392
Altamonte Springs Fl. 32716

Fresh Touch
—PUBLISHING—

© 2020 by Dr. Reno I. Johnson

All rights reserved solely by the author. The author guarantees all contents are original and do not infringe upon the legal rights of any other person or work. No part of this book may be reproduced in any form without the permission of the author. The views expressed in this book are not necessarily those of the publisher.

Unless otherwise indicated, Scripture quotations taken from the Modern English Version (MEV). Copyright © 2014 by Military Bible Association. Published and distributed by Charisma House. All rights reserved.

Scripture quotations taken from the King James Version (KJV) – *public domain*.

Printed in the United States of America.

ISBN-13: 978-1-6299-8548-0

CONTENTS

Introduction ix

Chapter One: The Pit 1

Chapter Two: The Party 23

Chapter Three: The Prison...................... 39

Chapter Four: The Palace....................... 59

Chapter Five: Born to Reign!.................... 87

Notes 107

About the Author.............................. 109

Contact the Author 111

INTRODUCTION

Joseph was a dreamer. The very call of God on his life started with a dream. When he was just a teenager, Joseph dreamed he would one day rule over all of his elder brothers and that they would bow before him, acknowledging him as their ruler. When Joseph revealed this dream to his brothers, it created tremendous upheaval between him and his siblings, spawning tumultuous, sorrowful, and shameful events throughout Joseph's family.

Yet God, in His sovereignty, had given Joseph his unusual dream and would use the tragic family drama that it caused to fulfill a high calling in Joseph's life. In His foreknowledge God had selected him for a great destiny: *Joseph was born to reign.*

The young man would, in time, rise up to occupy the second highest office in the nation of Egypt—which at that time in history was unmatched anywhere in the world in governmental or military might. Egypt was the leading political, economic, and technological power of the world. Thus, Joseph would one day stand as the second most powerful man in the entire world, surpassed only by Pharaoh himself—for whom he acted as chief adviser.

In His foreknowledge, God knew a day was coming when a great famine would blanket the southeastern Mediterranean region. It would threaten to destroy most of the known world. His sovereign plan was to use Joseph, after first speaking to him through prophetic dreams, to spare the lives of countless men, women, children, and animals and bring glory to His name throughout the entire Egyptian empire.

But there was a second purpose for raising up Joseph to reign in Egypt. God was also setting the stage for the birth of the nation of Israel! It was that nation of people, Joseph being the first, that God would deliver out of Egypt centuries later through Moses and lead into the Promised Land.

The story of Joseph is one that all of us as believers in Jesus Christ need to know:

- Like Joseph, we too have been called by God to a high calling: "This one thing I do, forgetting those things which are behind and reaching forward to those things which are ahead, I press toward the goal to the prize of the high calling of God in Christ Jesus" (Phil. 3:13–15).

- Like Joseph, we too have been born to reign: "To Him who loved us and washed us from our sins in His own blood, and has made us kings and priests to His God and Father" (Rev. 1:5–6).

- Like Joseph, we too have to endure hardships so we can be found faithful: "You have persevered and have endured hardships for my name, and have not grown weary" (Rev. 2:3, NIV).

Introduction

Joseph shows us that the *palace*—not the *pit*—is where God plans to take us. We see that when His plan is to put us on top, He can't be stopped. We see that when we are born to reign, the enemy opposes us in vain. The story of Joseph teaches us this.

But before any of that could take place for Joseph, he, his brothers, and their father, Jacob (aka Israel), would have to learn obedience, humility, and brokenness before God. The high calling God had for them as a family demanded it.

Sometimes you have to be separated from people you love so God can do what He wants to do in your life. You have to pull away from them because they can't deal with what God is doing with you or what you are becoming. For some, jealously blinds them; and it's no longer about the relationship they had with you, it's about what you possess. They want it and can't have it, so they oppose you.

In order for the stage to be set for the fulfillment of Joseph's destiny, the young man would first have to endure years of separation from his family. Our redeeming God would turn that tragic time into one of the most miraculous stories of redemption in history. But first, Joseph, his brothers, and his father all would face sorrow, regret, and brokenness like they'd never known before.

That is where our story begins.

Chapter One

THE PIT

Pit (literal): A hole in the ground designed to serve as a trap into which wild animals may fall and so be captured...an area dug out or sunk into the ground as a place of imprisonment.

Pit (figurative): A season of great testing when fear, abandonment, financial loss, betrayal, or any other challenge to faith can cause a Christian to feel as if they are without hope, without strength, and forgotten by God (see Psalms 35:7 and 88:3–6).

> Now Joseph dreamed a dream, and when he told it to his brothers, they hated him.... And they took him and threw him into a pit.
> —Genesis 37:5, 24

THE BIBLE OPENS this story about Joseph when he was just a boy, only seventeen years old. He was a young man, a teenager, a maturing boy who was learning responsibility. His job was to feed his father's flock. Presumably he was a shepherd in training. But God had much bigger plans for Joseph's life.

The Bible says in Isaiah 55:8–9 that God's thoughts are

not our thoughts, nor are our ways His ways. God's will for Joseph's future was about to envelop young Joseph and utterly rewrite the story of his life; for the Lord was about to take the young shepherd out of the fields and put him into "the pit" where his faith would be tested. It would be his first step on the path to fulfilling God's will. Eventually it would lead Joseph to the palaces of Egypt—a world superpower in that day and time.

As we'll see later in this chapter, the pit was to Joseph a soul shocking floor of rocky dirt—a place of numbing rejection; cold, empty, foreign, and dead. But to God, whose ways are infinitely higher, that cold earth of the pit was the warm, rich soil where the seeds of Joseph's high calling were springing to life and the pit's hard rocks stepping stones to the throne of Pharaoh where God would use Joseph to keep His people alive (see Genesis 50:20).

If you are facing a dark, lonely time in your walk with God, let this fact give you hope: your pain (your "pit") has a God-ordained purpose in your life just as much as Joseph's pit had for his life.

Being entrusted with the flock was a responsibility Joseph took seriously. That's why when he saw his brothers doing things he knew were contrary to his father's values he felt he must report them.

> Joseph...was feeding the flock with his brothers, and the boy was with the sons of Bilhah and with the sons of Zilpah, his father's wives. Joseph brought back a bad report about them to their father.
> —GENESIS 37:2

Joseph was not trying to snitch on his brothers or betray them. He was trying to be committed and faithful in the assignment his father gave him.

Joseph wanted his father to know what his brothers were secretly doing because he knew the flock was very important to his father, Jacob (also known as Israel). The Bible is showing us that Joseph's character and abilities were superior to his brothers'.

Genesis 37 says Joseph was the son of Jacob's old age (v. 3). The Hebrew phrase here does not signify an actual age. In those days it underscored the quality of "wisdom." In other words, Israel looked upon Joseph as the wisest of all of his sons. He was the one whom he could empower or entrust with riches and responsibilities.

It's important to note that Benjamin was actually the youngest of Jacob's sons (see Genesis 35:21–26). Being the youngest, he should have been Israel's favorite son; but that significance was bestowed on Joseph. God is going to bless and use the people He knows will not allow His choice of them go to their heads. As we shall see, when Joseph knew that God had called him and chosen him, although he excitedly told his family about the future God had in store for him, he was innocent in his excitement. He was not proud, nor was he a braggart. He simply rejoiced over God's favor on his life and wanted to share his joy with the people he loved most.

The coat of many colors

Everyone around Joseph knew that Israel loved him deeply and favored him. In fact, Israel's heart for his beloved Joseph was so strong that he could not hide it, so he made a coat for Joseph. It was tailor-made; Bible scholars say it probably was full-length with long sleeves.

Coats of many colors were formed or fashioned by sewing together patches of colors or different colored swatches of cloth. They were a dress code of distinction. Parents in those days who dressed a child in extravagant attire did so because the child was special to them.

A colorful coat was a symbol of prosperity. It separated the individual who wore one from anyone who didn't. It symbolized Joseph's authority and favor for all to see.

In the same way, God has placed a coat of many colors on you. He is not going to hide what He intends for you or how He feels about you. God has you on display, too.

A coat of many colors will draw attention, good and bad. The fact that the Father is openly blessing you and pouring out His favor on you is going to attract attacks from people you'd least expect to be opposed to you.

Peace—deserved but denied

This is what happened to Joseph. Verse 4 says his brothers could not speak "peaceably" to Joseph.

> But when his brothers saw that their father loved him more than all his brothers, they hated him and could not speak peaceably to him.
> —Genesis 37:4

What does it mean to "speak peaceably"? In those days the usual expression of good wishes among friends and acquaintances was: "Peace be to you." It was the expression used when they'd see one another on the street. It was a way of speaking love and blessing over another person.

To "speak peaceably" to someone was deemed a sacred or holy duty. If you believed in Jehovah God, it was considered a sacred obligation when you walked by a person that you would say, "Peace be to you, my friend." It was a sign that you were in covenant with God and had a relationship with Him. It meant you recognized God as your father and that person as your brother or your sister.

To withhold the greeting was a sign of dislike or hidden hostility. It symbolized opposition. It indicated that one person held resentment or an aggression toward the other person.

Joseph never heard those words, "peace be to you," from his brothers. They refused to love on him at all. Their habitual refusal to greet Joseph with the customary salutation showed how ill-disposed they were toward him. They simply could not stand him. No matter what Joseph said or did, they found fault with him. I'm certain you are familiar with this experience in your own life to some degree; but know that it's all because people envy the favor of God on you.

When jealousy is present, the peace that is *deserved* is *denied*. Some folks just won't celebrate you. They will never tell you about the good they see in you. Therefore, you must learn how to encourage yourself in the Lord. David did this during a time when he was deeply discouraged by the way people were bitterly treating him. First Samuel 30:6 says that he "encouraged himself in the Lord."

Imagine Joseph having to sit in the house at the table with his brothers and they would not speak peaceably to him. They would speak to each other when they dined but not say a kind word to Joseph. The only reason for this was the favor of God. It was wrapped around Joseph just like his multicolored coat. And they were jealous of it.

Jealousy is dangerous. It can lead people to act in despicable ways you never imagined they would (as we will see with Joseph's brothers). We might encounter jealousy anywhere. It happens in church. It happens on the job. It happens between sisters and brothers. It happens between husbands and wives. Jealousy is like a predator that's out to devour the thing it wants most.

You see, when God starts to bless us, we will battle extreme warfare. It can get difficult, especially when the people we think we know actually have their fingers crossed in hope that we will crash and burn. When you have been born to reign, the peace you deserved is denied; but that doesn't stop God from moving on your behalf.

Favored and hated

You may be in a season when every time you turn around it seems like there is something knocking at your door that you don't want to deal with. Joseph had the same experience. He opened the door, thinking his family's love for him was knocking; but he found out it was their hate. You might be saying: "Every time I try to do good, evil presents itself. Every time I try to move forward, my good intention is misunderstood and people turn it into evil."

Do you know why that happens? Because you are *distinct*. Deep in their spirits, those people know there is something special about you. The Father's coat is on you, and that is why they oppose you. The Father has dressed you and caused them to see that you are chosen by Him. And guess what? It doesn't matter what the enemy attempts to do in order to *undo* what God has done in your life because he can't touch it. It is the Father's work, and the enemy has no right to it or say in it.

We see in Genesis 37:4 that Joseph's brothers hated him when they saw the coat and understood that their father loved Joseph more than them. Joseph had done nothing to them; he hadn't wronged them in any way, he was just being favored by his father. But his brothers knew what his beautiful coat symbolized, and they hated him all the more for it.

If you have been favored by God like Joseph was, and folks are opposing you for it, know this: At the end of the day, your pit is just the preparation for your palace. God knows that every trial you experience is for your betterment. *Every fire that you pass through has been tailor-made to develop you.* Joseph faced the pit; but in all of that, God was equipping him to reign. *My friend, enjoy the favor and ignore the haters because your God has the last say—and according to the Father you are favored. You are born to reign!*

Joseph the Dreamer

> Now Joseph dreamed a dream, and when he told it to his brothers, they hated him even more. He said to them, "Please listen to this dream which I have dreamed. We were binding sheaves in the field. All of a sudden my sheaf rose up and stood upright, and your sheaves stood around it and bowed down to my sheaf." His brothers said to him, "Will you really reign over us, or will you really have dominion over us?" So they hated him even more because of his dreams and his words.
> —Genesis 37:5–8

Dreams in ancient times were greatly respected and closely observed. The dream Joseph had drew some serious attention from his family.

There are times when you sense in your spirit that God is about to do some wonderful things in your life. You find that God even confirms what you are sensing—using a vision, dream, or word of knowledge to ignite your faith. Filled with excitement, you rush out to tell those around you that God is about to do wonders in your life. But then, to your surprise, your joy and newfound vision birth hate. Because of the jealousy and fear in the hearts of those people, they despise you.

I believe questions arose among Joseph's brothers after Joseph told them about the future plans God had for his life. Here's what I think was running through their minds: "What if that really happens? What if God really opens the door for him to rule over us? What if God really does this like Joseph says He is going to? What will happen to *us*?"

Joseph was so innocent. He thought he could tell his brothers personal things about his life. He believed his brothers had his back—that they were on his side. Naturally he wanted to tell them what he had dreamed. For Joseph it was an exciting thing to realize, but for his brothers it created misery. Your enemies are saying, "Kill the dreamer!" But God is saying, "Keep the dream alive."

Celebrating Joseph was not what his brothers were thinking about doing. Their hearts already were stirring with thoughts of how to stop Joseph and keep his dream from becoming a reality. They didn't admit it to him right then, but they were seriously threatened by his dream.

Wow! That's exactly what people are saying about you: they are asking what will happen if God does what He has showed you He plans to do. If this happens to you, don't be alarmed. *Just as God created and ordained the sun to shine, so He has created and ordained you to shine. God will do what He has showed you. But remember: no pit, no palace.*

Not only could Joseph's brothers not stop God's plan,

I believe God employed them right there on the spot to help make it happen! He saw their thoughts and put them on an assignment right then and there. Their assignment (though they weren't aware of it) was to help get Joseph right where God wanted him to go.

The same goes for you: *The people you think should be with you might not be; but they are the very ones God is going to use to get you to where He is taking you.*

Think about Joseph in relation to God's divine providence. *Divine providence* is the daily, constant, sovereign, independent rule of God over all things in the universe for the accomplishment of His perfect will. The doctrine of divine providence affirms that God is in complete control of all things. It says: "It is not by coincidence that you're here. God is in control. You are supposed to be here."

Because God is in control of everything, this passage tells me that Joseph dreamed a dream from God and, in God's providential schedule, told his brothers about the dream so that they would do the very thing God needed them to do—which was to get Joseph closer to his destiny! (Later in this chapter, we will see how this worked out.)

So I believe by divine providence that God also allowed Joseph to tell his brothers what he dreamed, even though Joseph's brothers hated him and were opposed to his success.

And the Bible says he simply told them his dream—they were the ones who interpreted it. But they deciphered it correctly—they knew what it meant for them. Notice that their hatred for Joseph only mounted as a result of it. Now they hated him not just for being the favorite son and wearing the coat of honor but also for his dream and for saying they would bow down to him. That was the last thing they wanted to do—or intended to do.

Adding insult to injury

> Then he dreamed another dream and told it to his brothers and said, "I have dreamed another dream. The sun and the moon and eleven stars were bowing to me."
> —Genesis 37:9

They hadn't gotten over the first dream—and now Joseph was telling them about a second one that *again* described how he was going to rule over them. The new dream went a step further. It said even his parents would bow down to him!

If I were to tell you about a breakthrough in my life and see great displeasure in your countenance as a result, it would be unwise of me to come back to you a second time and tell you about another good thing that was about to happen for me. But God needed for Joseph's brothers to hate him to the point of wanting to destroy him so that He could use the pain they inflicted on Joseph to process the young man for his promise.

The pit would make him fit for the fulfillment of his dreams! God had plans to take Joseph to the palace, no matter what the course of his life looked like at that point.

Maybe you need to seize that truth about God for yourself. God has a plan to take you to your destiny, but you aren't given the privilege of choosing which vehicle or road He will use to get you there. Know this: *God's plan for your life is always executed in the wisest manner possible; therefore, He will get you there. Stay in the vehicle and ignore the road He takes, even if the road gets rough.* As I said before, *your pit has a purpose.*

Joseph felt like everyone wanted to see him succeed. Not so. Little did he know that the very people he lived with didn't just want him to fail; they soon were going to want him dead. But they couldn't stop what God had started. The one whom God has blessed can't be cursed.

Yes, it hurts sometimes when you discover who doesn't want to see you get to the top. Yes, it's difficult to deal with. But I guarantee that if you hang on, you will have victory over every opposition.

Genesis 37:9 says that Joseph told his family, "Behold, the sun and the moon and the eleven stars made obeisance to me" (KJV). Joseph was adding insult to injury. *Obeisance* is the moving of the body in such a way as to express deep respect or differential courtesy, as before a superior. It means to bow or to make a similar gesture.

When the favor of God is on you, all you have to do is please God and He will do the rest. Nothing bothers people more than when they have done their best to get you in their grip and you slip through:

- They were certain you were going to fail—but you prevailed.

- They were certain you were going to get discouraged—but you stood your ground and found hope.

- They were certain you were going down—but God lifted you up.

Joseph's brothers believed he was arrogant, egotistical, and big headed. Have you ever tried to tell somebody about something good that is happening for you but their response just makes you shut down? They make you feel like your "good thing" isn't welcome with them.

But if you read the passage in Genesis for what it says,

you understand that Joseph wasn't being arrogant. He just loved his brothers and was excited to share with them what God was going to do for him. Why? Because he knew that when God blessed him, they would also be blessed.

Joseph was simply sharing his sense of destiny with anyone who would listen; he just wanted a listening ear. It's hard when you have something so exciting to tell someone but you don't have a listening ear. The very people Joseph wanted to share his heart with the most didn't want him to have what he had dreamed. Now they had to deal with his favor *and* his dream—adding insult to injury. They were opposed to his success because they envied him. The pit!

Envy means "covetousness with regard to another's advantages, success, or possessions."[1] It's a "painful or resentful awareness of an advantage enjoyed by another, accompanied by a desire to possess the same advantage."[2]

Envy creates a compelling, sometimes irresistible desire to have something that belongs to another person. You know you need a spiritual flushing when you will go to any extent necessary to take what belongs to somebody else so you can enjoy it for yourself! That's envy in action!

Joseph experienced envy in the highest degree from his brothers, but yet envy could not overpower destiny. Born to reign!

JOSEPH THE (FUTURE) PRINCE

> But when he told it to his father and his brothers, his father rebuked him and said to him, "What is this dream that you have dreamed? Will I and your mother and your brothers really come to bow down ourselves to you to the ground?" So his brothers

The Pit

were jealous of him, but his father kept the matter in mind.
—Genesis 37:10–11

The Bible tells us that Jacob rebuked his son when he heard about his second dream. Maybe he was okay with Joseph's first dream, since it only mentioned Joseph's brothers. But now Joseph was saying something Jacob didn't want to hear. He asked Joseph: "Will I and your mother and your brothers really come to bow down ourselves to you?"

Was he offended? Probably. In not so many words, he was chastising Joseph, saying: "This thing is not possible, so get it out of your head. This so-called dream you had is foolishness. Do you think your mother and I are going to bow to the ground to you? I don't think so."

Could it be that when Jacob heard about the dream he almost tipped over too? At the least he shot a fiery arrow of discouragement at Joseph. Jealousy is a dangerous thing. It sounds like even Jacob was becoming jealous of Joseph. But no matter what, Joseph was the future prince.

The Bible also says Jacob "kept the matter in mind." In other words, Israel paid attention because he knew the track record of God. He knew that God's ways were higher than his; and he knew from personal experience that when God spoke a word, He would watch over it to bring it to pass. *Get ready, because God is about to release something in your future that is going to change your status!*

Joseph the Obedient

Now his brothers went to feed their father's flock in Shechem. Israel said to Joseph, "Are not your brothers feeding the flock in Shechem? Come, and

> I will send you to them." He answered, "Here I am." Israel said to him, "Please go and see if it is well with your brothers and well with the flocks, and bring back word to me."...So Joseph went after his brothers and found them in Dothan. When they saw him some distance away, before he came near to them, they conspired against him to kill him.
> —Genesis 37:12–14, 17–18

Joseph was so pure and so full of love that his brothers had to go some fifty miles from home to get away from him! They used the excuse that the family flock would find better pasture elsewhere. Anxious to learn how his sons were doing in their distant encampment, Jacob dispatched Joseph to find them and bring him news. Joseph accepted the mission eagerly; he was excited to obey his father. Jacob of course had no idea what he was sending Joseph into.

But I have news for you: God knew. Jacob did not know he was putting his beloved son in mortal danger, but God knew it; and it was right where He needed Joseph to go.

When it seems like God is giving you some strange instructions that are taking you away from what He has said concerning you, don't let the enemy steal your faith. His instructions are not actually taking you away from your assignment; they are bringing you into it. When things look contrary to what God is saying, you'd better watch closely because God is at work. In time, He will hasten His Word to perform it (Jer. 1:12).

Think about it this way: Right after Joseph dreamed his dreams—right after God's powerful words of destiny had come to him—God sent him on a one-way trip toward a pit of captivity in the wilderness! Now, the story would be different if Joseph had gone off on his own and trouble had befallen him. But that was not the case. He was obeying his father.

You will always experience a rough and tough season before God elevates you. Like it was with Joseph, your dream will end up endangered before you get to the top.

God knows exactly what you are going to experience, exactly what you're going to pass through, and exactly what instruments He will use to prepare you. Be encouraged— He also knows you're going to come forth as pure gold that has been tried in the fire.

Destined for destiny

So here goes Joseph, heading toward his brothers who hate him for his beautiful coat (which he is wearing!) and who think he is egotistical, arrogant, and big headed. The only thing that comes to their minds when they see him in the distance is that they have to get rid of him! Even before he had come near to them, they conspired against him.

I mentioned previously that this is similar to how people may treat you. They sense in their hearts there is something significant about you, that your future is as bright as the sun, and they therefore conspire against you. Sometimes God even gives people a sneak preview of your future; they can see where you're headed and they want to stop you before you get there. You wonder: "Why are they fighting me? Why are they coming against me?" It's because when you are marked by God people notice it even before you do. Therefore, for those who are your oppositions, the urge in their hearts is: "I must stop them before they get to their destiny." Destined for destiny!

Don't be surprised when you are opposed. People who

have the mind-set if they can't have it, then you can't have it will go to any limit to block you; this is what Joseph was about to experience. But the Bible promises us that the steps of a good man are "ordered." Ordered by whom? *By the Lord* (see Psalm 37:23). Joseph wasn't walking into a trap. He was walking on a road to the palace!

Like Joseph, you may have to pass through some rough stuff first, but I guarantee you, God will get you to the palace. You're destined for destiny!

The Pit before the Palace

> They said one to another, "The master of dreams comes! Come now, let us kill him and throw him into some pit, and we will say, 'Some evil beast has devoured him.' Then we will see what will become of his dreams." But when Reuben heard it, he rescued him out of their hands, saying, "Let us not kill him." Reuben said to them, "...throw him into this pit here in the wilderness."
> —Genesis 37:19–22

Being called a "master of dreams" was a bitterly ironical statement. It meant that Joseph's brothers regarded him as an artful, deceitful pretender. When Joseph told them his dreams one after another, they mocked him for dreaming—for just *having* a dream. They were sarcastic about it. In effect they were saying, "This foolish dreamer is pretending. Nothing is going to happen for him, so don't worry. But, just in case, let's put him in this pit to *make sure* it doesn't happen." *They didn't know that the pit was Joseph's elevator to the palace!*

Folks may have thrown you into a pit—not a physical hole in the ground, of course, but an emotional or a spiritual pit. Many times the Bible uses the word *pit* figuratively to describe a season of great testing when we feel as if we're in a prison. It symbolizes a season in which you feel like you're fumbling in the dark, without hope, without strength, and forgotten by God (see Psalms 35:7; 38:1-8; 88:3-6). It can represent a season when you experience loneliness, fear, abandonment, a loss of finances, a betrayal of trust, a setback in your faith, or any other trial of life that tests you to your limits.

Maybe this has happened to you before, or maybe it's something you are living through right now. Is someone scandalizing your name, blocking your progress, attacking you for no reason? If so, then you need to know this for certain that *your pit is your elevator to something greater.*

The Bible says that Reuben stopped his brothers from killing Joseph. He talked them into putting him in the pit instead of murdering him. Whenever God has a purpose, He has a plan. Because of *purpose*, God used Reuben to make sure that Joseph didn't die. But because of *plan*, He allowed Joseph to experience the pit. The same may apply to you: *The pit is coming before the palace.*

The psalmist declared, "They have prepared a net for my steps; my soul is bowed down; they have dug a pit before me" (Ps. 57:6). With some people, the only thing they are concerned about is that nothing good happens for you. As long as you don't have anything, as long as nothing good is going on in your life, then you don't pose a threat to them. But as soon as the cloud of glory comes over you, the fight begins.

Joseph never expected to be in a battle with his brothers; and I am certain that after being thrown into the pit, he thought he was finished. You may be in a pit, but I can guarantee you you're not finished; it's definitely not the end of you. Like I have always said, "Jealousy is a terrible infection, but success is a no-nonsense antibiotic that will kill it." *Get ready to reign!*

The passage goes on to say:

> When Joseph came to his brothers, they stripped Joseph of his coat—his coat of many colors that he had on. And they took him and threw him into a pit.
> —GENESIS 37:23–24

Their eyes were on what? The coat! The first thing they did was strip Joseph of his coat. They were spitefully dealing with him over two dreams, but then this brother of theirs also was wearing *the coat*. This special coat clearly stated that Joseph was like royalty; he was blessed and favored and much more. All this caused his brothers to hate him, tremble in fear at the sight of him, and grow increasingly eager to get rid of him. Favor frustrates people to the point that they will hate you, fear you, and even do everything in their power to get rid of you.

They took away Joseph's coat, but they couldn't take away his call! What they took away was the natural coat, just a symbol of what Joseph was wearing in the Spirit. They messed up because they thought that if they took it away then Joseph could not have what God had promised him. How wrong they were!

Some of you have been stripped of your coat, just like Joseph was. You once were wearing a coat of many colors that symbolized the Father's favor, but the attacks of the enemy have shaken your faith. *Know this: the coat was only an earthly sign with a heavenly meaning that will manifest in the fullness of time. Your pit has a purpose!*

The enemy can never stop what God has ordained for

you, so in the end the dream will become a reality. People may not literally see your colorful or prosperous coat right now; but they know it's there, they know you're going to prosper. You may look bare, you may look uncovered, you may look unprotected, you may look like you're alone, you may look like a failure because of the season that you're in; but according to heaven it's only a matter of time before what your coat represented, represents you. In other words, favor is about to stand up for you!

The coat was not the actual favor of God upon Joseph, but a symbol of His favor, representing what God had ordained for Joseph. It is much like the oil used by the prophet Samuel to anoint David as king over Israel (see 1 Samuel 16:1-13). The oil only symbolized God's anointing upon David. It wasn't his actual anointing. The anointing to rule Israel was spiritual—and it would manifest later, in God's time. In the meantime, however, it didn't matter who came against David to thwart his course to the throne. God had chosen him and anointed him, and David would eventually become king.

In the same way, it didn't matter how they came against Joseph because he was already favored by God! *At the end of the day, you too will make it to the top even after your experience at the bottom (the pit)!*

Let this encourage you to stay willing to go through your own process. God is moving you from symbolism to reality, from the promise to the fulfillment, from "signs" to "wonders." The coat was a "sign" of the "wonder" God had bestowed upon Joseph's life.

By putting Joseph in a pit with no food or water, his brothers were expecting him to die. That's cruel. I would rather be hit with a sudden blow than put in a pit in the wilderness and allowed to suffer. But the choice isn't mine to make—or yours—since it is God who controls the heat of His refiner's fire. It's plain to see that everybody but Reuben wanted Joseph to perish. God will always place a Reuben in your life because of *purpose*.

They were putting Joseph through so much torment, and what they were doing didn't even touch their conscience because all they cared about was that Joseph perished. All they could think was, "If it isn't me God blesses, then it sure isn't going to be him."

The pit had no water, the pit had no food, and it was known in those days that the pits were snaky. Many of you understand this as it relates to your own life. The pit is a hard place in life, and you know what it's like to be in it. Being thrown into a pit like Joseph was, out of jealousy, must be a pain without a name—indescribable.

Everyone's pit is different, but you must survive when you find yourself in one.

Maybe your pit is knowing what it's like to be attacked, especially by those you least expected; or to face depression or physical pain or loneliness or rejection or betrayal. Any of those things, and many more, could be your pit. When you're there, you feel alone, like no one is there with you. Sometimes you feel so alone that you wonder if God is still with you. But, of course, He's there. He's just a God of timing.

Hebrews 13:5 exhorts us: "For He has said: 'I will never leave you, nor forsake you.'"

The enemy wants you to feel like he is winning. By taking Joseph away from his earthly father, his brothers were unknowingly placing him in the hands of his heavenly Father that He might prepare him for what He had promised him. In the same way, *when you are experiencing the pit, please don't quit. God knows exactly where you're going and which road is best to get you there. Declare this: "I'm in the pit but I refuse to quit!"*

Yes, the pit is unpleasant. But knowing that we were born to reign helps us endure the pain. It doesn't matter who is conspiring against you. The only thing that can happen to you is what God allows—and whatever God allows to happen to you is good for you.

As the Scripture says in Psalm 40:2: "He also brought me up out of a horrible pit, out of the miry clay, and set my feet on a rock, and established my steps."

What are your enemies going to do after they have thrown you in the pit and realize that your pit has a purpose? *Your pit will make you fit. Fit to rule. For you were born to reign!*

In the next chapter we will see God perform His Word for Joseph and lead him another step closer to the fulfillment of his dreams.

Chapter Two

THE PARTY

Party (literal): A social gathering or assembly of persons for entertainment, amusement, or pleasure.

Party (figurative): A celebration that features food and beverages. In many cultures, it is customary to throw a farewell party for someone who is departing on a long trip.

> And they took him and threw him into a pit. The pit was empty, and there was no water in it. Then they sat down to eat.
> —Genesis 37:24–25

Joseph the Slave

We saw in chapter 1 that Joseph was openly loved and favored by his father, Israel. As a symbol of his favor and love for Joseph, Israel made him a coat of many colors. It signified to all who saw it that Joseph bore the distinction, authority, favor, and blessing of his father. It made his brothers very jealous when they saw that their father loved Joseph more than them.

We also saw that Joseph had two very important prophetic dreams, one right after the other. In the first one he became the ruler over his brothers (who all were older). In the second dream he became ruler over his entire family, including his parents. When he excitedly told his family about these good things the Lord had shown him, his father became angry with him and his brothers' jealousy toward him turned to hatred and thoughts of murder.

We saw that in order to get away from Joseph, his brothers took the family's flocks of sheep to a distant pasture and stayed away from home for some time. When Israel became worried about his sons, he sent Joseph to find them and he directed Joseph to report back to him about their welfare and the condition of the flocks.

We saw that when Joseph finally found his brothers camping in a distant wilderness area, they conspired together to do him harm. All of them except Reuben wanted to murder him. But God used Reuben to spare Joseph's life. The brothers instead threw Joseph into a deep pit used by hunters to trap wild game.

It amazes me that as we walk this Christian journey it will so often take an unexpected turn, often immediately after God makes an amazing liberating promise to us or in some other way significantly blesses us. No sooner has God prophetically given you a dream or used a prophet to speak a joyous blessing over your life, then, *boom!* everything in your world starts to deteriorate!

Why is that?

As Christians—as born-again believers and followers of the Lord Jesus Christ—we need to understand that the disciple is not greater than his master. "The disciple is not above his teacher, nor the servant above his master" (Matt. 10:24). The Bible tells us that Jesus, even though He was the Son of God, had to learn obedience by the things He suffered: "Though he was a Son, He learned obedience through the things that He suffered" (Heb. 5:8).

Joseph was no different. After dreaming such awesome dreams, he would have to suffer before he can reign. He would have to become totally yielded to God. This was necessary before God could raise him up and seat him in one of the highest positions of power in the world—at the right hand of Pharaoh.

But for now, he had to be seated in a pit while he listened to a party being held to celebrate his demise!

A Crazy Party

> Then they sat down to eat. And looking up, they saw a caravan of Ishmaelites coming from Gilead, with their camels bearing spices, balm, and myrrh, carrying it down to Egypt. Then Judah said to his brothers, "What profit is it if we kill our brother and cover up his blood? Come, let us sell him to the Ishmaelites, and let us not lay our hand on him, for he is our brother and our own flesh." So his brothers agreed.
> —Genesis 37:25–27

Due to their extreme jealousy, which had turned into hatred, Joseph's brothers not only had no conscience about tossing their brother into a hole in the ground to rot, they also had no problem turning right around and having themselves a little party to celebrate their good fortune. Joseph would finally be out of their way!

Finally they would not have to put up with seeing Joseph favored and treated like royalty by their father. Finally they would not have to watch Joseph get the first place in everything while they sat by getting the second place.

Wow, it's amazing what people will do to get rid of you! But the good news for you and me is that if God has begun a good work in us, then no one can stop it. Let them have their party, let them celebrate, because at the end of the day they will realize that it's too late—you've already been blessed.

They knew Joseph had no water or food in that pit and that it was possible that snakes or other dangerous predators could have been in the pit. All they wanted to know was that Joseph was out of their way. The party!

While their own brother was in the pit fighting for his life, they were right there having a feast, having a crazy party. Sounds like your story, right? *Folks will do anything to block you so that you won't prosper—and then they'll stand back and watch you suffer while they party, all because of jealousy.*

Well, while they are watching you, God is watching them, and it's just a matter of time before your process becomes your promise. What an amazing God we serve! I'm in a pit; they are having a party; but at the end of the day my pit elevated me to the palace and their party took them down to the pit. Go ahead. Have your party. I will endure for the palace!

The Word of God admonishes us that we are not to rejoice when our enemies fall: "Do not rejoice when your enemy falls, and do not let your heart be glad when he stumbles" (Prov. 24:17). How much more then should we not rejoice when our own brothers or sisters are in pain? But Joseph's brothers had so little conscience about what they were doing to their own brother that while Joseph was fighting for his life down in the pit they were up top having a great time!

That is almost too crazy to imagine. Can you picture your own family members sitting around a picnic table outside your burning house, talking, laughing, and

The Party

grilling while you are inside fighting for your life trying to get out of the fire? Is that not crazy? That's the mind-set these men had toward their brother, all because of jealousy.

What makes his situation even more tragic is that Joseph trusted his brothers with all his heart. But his trust was misplaced. They failed him miserably. The Bible warns us against trusting in the "arm of flesh" (2 Chron. 32:8)—which means to trust in people and what they can do for you more than you trust in the Lord. The reason God warns us against doing this is that the arm of flesh will fail you:

> Cursed is the man who trusts in man and makes flesh his strength, and whose heart departs from the Lord.
> —Jeremiah 17:5

Man will fail you but God, however, will never fail you. For the Scripture declares, "Whoever believes in Him will not be disappointed" (Rom. 10:11, nas).

The Bible says that after Joseph was thrown into the pit his brothers looked up and saw the Ishmaelites coming. Perfect timing! They realized this was their way out—they could sell Joseph and wouldn't have to kill him or leave him in the pit to die. "Let's wrap up our party with a sale!" they probably said. "We'll make some good money on the side by selling Joseph to them. We'll go home with cash in our pockets—one more reason for us to celebrate!"

And that's what they did. They sold their own brother as a slave for twenty pieces of silver. They handed him over to total strangers to take him into a foreign land and do whatever they wanted with him.

If that isn't a crystal clear way of saying, "We don't ever want to see you again, Joseph! Good riddance!" then I don't know what is. And it all was because God had promised Joseph a future that they couldn't stand the thought of seeing come to pass.

The Bible says, "Anger is cruel and fury overwhelming, but who can stand before jealousy?" (Prov. 27:4, NIV). The spirit of jealousy is so serious. If you are tempted to let it operate in your life, *don't*! If you covet something your neighbor has, first repent of that sin and then cry out to God to provide your need. But don't open the door to jealousy or envy.

In Genesis 4:3–8 we see that jealousy led Cain into a life of crime. It was the spirit of envy and jealously that tempted Cain until he gave in and murdered his own brother. Cain killed Abel because God *favored* Abel.

The same thing almost happened with Joseph's brothers. They didn't kill Joseph, but their jealousy inspired them to commit a crime.

Dream Killers

As far as the big picture was concerned, it's doubtful Joseph could have made a connection between what he was going through and what God had promised him. His dreams had not revealed enough details for him to know how God intended to raise him up. He didn't yet see the connection between the pit, the party, and the palace. I'll often tell people: "The best road to your destiny is the one that God chooses. Through all the bumps, He will get you there!"

Besides, at that moment, Joseph was dealing with some serious dream killers. What do you think he might have been feeling, sitting there in a hole in the ground listening to his brothers eating, laughing, and enjoying themselves up top? For one thing, he felt something sinking into his bones that was colder than the dirt and rocks in the bottom of that pit.

He felt betrayal setting in. He was beginning to realize this was no joke. His brothers weren't kidding around. This was not some sort of warped stunt or trick they were playing on him. They meant to do him serious harm. He was beginning to understand that he had suddenly been thrust into the midst of a severe trial. His brothers hadn't killed his body, but because of what they had done to him the emotional innocence of his youth was slowly being put to death.

Remember, he was only seventeen years old; and from everything the Scripture tells us about him we can surmise that he was an obedient, respectful, happy, loyal, resilient, and family oriented young man. While his brothers were partying together up top, he was alone down below suffering the devastating pain of emotional death. He was going through the loss of love, family, trust, and childlike faith in those he believed were his best friends—all at one time. When you think about it, the cruelty of his brothers' party is almost unreal.

Dream killers had surrounded Joseph, above and below. While his brothers celebrated his demise and the end of any chance he might have to see his dreams fulfilled, he quietly faced the deep wounds of betrayal and the lie that he was losing forever everything that was dear to him.

But if Joseph could have heard God speaking to him right then or could have known God's thoughts toward him at that dire moment in his life, he would have heard the Lord saying:

> *Joseph, I am going to separate you that I might connect you. I will let your now die that your latter might live. You will be divided so that you might multiply. You will be bruised that you might be used. You will weep that you might rejoice. You will overcome hatred that you might lead reconciliation. You cannot understand all of this now. But in time you will. I will take you through the fire so I can take you higher. I have to put you between a rock and a hard place before I raise you to the high place.*

In the coming chapters of this book we will see how God fulfilled all of this in Joseph's life.

Waiting on the Lord

> They took Joseph's coat and killed a young goat and dipped the coat in the blood. Then they took the coat of many colors and brought it to their father and said, "This we have found. Do you know whether it is your son's robe or not?" He knew it and said, "It is my son's coat. A wild beast has devoured him. Joseph has without a doubt been torn into pieces."
> —Genesis 37:31–33

The Bible says Joseph's brothers put the goat's blood all over the coat to deceive their father into believing Joseph was dead. It was as if it were a symbol that everything the coat represented was dead. His beloved status with his father was gone. His mantle of favor had been stripped from him and bloodied.

Some of you feel the same way. You're saying: "I'm going through so much. I've lost everything I had. Everyone I thought was my friend has turned against me. None of this is adding up with what God has said about me."

Even if you are struggling, it doesn't mean that you are not on the right track. It means that God is preparing you for the promise. We see this in Joseph's life. Things were tough for him, but we see that God was hiding His plans under the radar while He got Joseph ready for the future—for the time when He would reveal His will to the brothers, Jacob, and the entire world. *So, take heart, there is a word over your life too, and the word will sustain you.*

Perhaps you have endured some hard times and now you find yourself trying to run away from God. The test has been hard, and you want to get away from it. Maybe God has made promises to you, but everything you're going through seems to be working against those promises. Maybe you've gotten tired—you don't want to push anymore, and you can't stop asking God, "Why am I going through all of this?"

Some of you are just like Joseph—your back is against the wall, you have no one else to turn to. You *have* to depend on God. You *have* to trust God to take you out of what you have been in for so long. You know now that you *have* to wait on God.

Be encouraged. The Bible declares:

> He gives power to the faint, and to those who have no might He increases strength. Even the youths shall faint and be weary, and the young men shall utterly fall, but those who wait upon the Lord shall renew their strength; they shall mount up with wings as eagles, they shall run and not be weary, and they shall walk and not faint.
> —Isaiah 40:29–31

You are an eagle being prepared to fly higher. You can't fly low anymore. God wants you to go higher, and He's giving you new wings that will enable you to soar. You are not a chicken pecking the ground in the barnyard. You are an eagle, and your wings are expanding. Here are six things you can do while you wait on God to renew your strength:

1. Stand in faith.

You and I cannot figure God out. We can't see all of what He is doing, just as Joseph couldn't. The Bible says His Word is a "lamp" to our feet: "Your word is a lamp to my feet and a light to my path" (Ps. 119:105).

It doesn't say it's a spotlight. If we could see everything all at once, we wouldn't need God! We wouldn't need His help or have to live by faith. And without faith, we'd truly be nowhere because without faith we cannot please God (Heb. 11:6).

Some of you were surprised when right after you received your promise you went through the fire. No matter what you are going through, you need to believe God is still at work bringing about the plans He has for your life. *You need to stand in faith that things are going to turn around in your favor.*

You need to say to God:

> *Lord, I'm still dreaming because I know You are calling me higher. I can't die because You can't lie. Something great is coming to me. I can smell victory. I can smell the rain coming that will make my life bloom again. I may be in a pit while everyone else is partying; but I know that Your Word, God, is going to take me to the palace.*

2. Don't settle for second-best.

Resist the temptation to go after what God is trying to get rid of. Don't try to go back to where God has taken you from because you think that place was better for you than the place you're in today. It wasn't!

Maybe you are fighting to go back yet you're finding that everything you try is going wrong. God's trying to tell you, you can't go back! God is trying to hold you in place for what He has for you tomorrow, not for what you had yesterday.

Even if you can hear the dream killers having their party while you're suffering in the pit, know that they can't stop God! They can *celebrate*, but they can't *terminate*—not when it comes to what God has planned for you.

Whatever you are going through, God is using it to take you where He intends for you to go. Hosea 6:2 says: "After two days will He revive us. On the third day He will raise us up, that we may live before Him."

There is a set time when God is going to bring you to that prepared place. Can you hold on until then? *Don't Settle for second best; but rather wait, because God is never late!*

3. Let God be in charge.

Don't try to help God out as you're waiting on Him. Maybe you have done this and are weighed down because things got worse. Remember, you and I are not as wise as God; therefore His way is always the best way. He knows exactly how much heat it will take for us to shine. Determine that you will wait on His perfect will.

Jeremiah 29:11 promises: "For I know the thoughts that I think toward you, saith the Lord, thoughts of peace, and not of evil, to give you an expected end" (KJV).

The thoughts God had for Joseph literally dug him up! They brought him up out of the pit and delivered him from the mockery of the party! Likewise, the thoughts that God has for you will dig you up from your pit. His thoughts will find you, in His perfect time. *Let God be in charge!*

4. Guard your heart.

Proverbs 4:23 says "Guard your heart above all else, for it determines the course of your life" (NLT). You have to do this not only when you are enduring the pit and the party but also when God has delivered you from both. At that time you may be tempted to mock, scorn, or revel in your triumph over your "enemies," but choose rather to go God's way by not rejoicing in their outcome. Choose instead to rejoice in God. Don't become bitter; become better. *Guard your heart!*

5. Be a worshiper.

Take time to worship. No matter what you are going through, when the burden of life weighs you down, if you will lift your hands and worship God every weight will come off of you.

Paul and Silas worshiped the Lord in the midst of their affliction, and He supernaturally broke their chains and set them free:

> At midnight Paul and Silas were praying and singing hymns to God, and the prisoners were listening to them. Suddenly there was a great earthquake, so that the foundations of the prison were shaken. And immediately all the doors were opened and everyone's shackles were loosened.
> —Acts 16:25–26

The Party

Worshipping God during a pit experience will get you a sure ticket to the palace. *While you are going through the furnace of affliction, be a worshiper.*

6. Praise God in all situations.

Praise God no matter what. Refuse to doubt Him. Refuse the devil's temptation to accuse Him. Can you still praise God when you can hear those who threw you in the pit having a party?

Yes.

Can you still lift your hands and say: "Lord, I know that all things are going to work together for my good. I know that You are going to bring to pass everything You promised me"?

Yes.

Can you praise God despite your temporary circumstances and how you feel?

Yes.

The Bible says that "weeping" endures only for a short time: "Weeping may endure for a night, but joy comes in the morning" (Ps. 30:5). That means you *can* praise God because joy is on the way! Let His praise be continually in your mouth, as Psalm 34:1 says; and, as Philippians 4:4 says, "Rejoice in the Lord always."

God does not show up to pity parties. But He loves to come to praise parties! Therefore, *praise Him in all situations.*

THE STEPS OF A GOOD MAN

> Meanwhile the Midianites sold him in Egypt to Potiphar, an officer of Pharaoh and captain of the guard.
> —GENESIS 37:36

The Bible says Joseph was taken into Egypt and sold to Potiphar, a high-ranking military officer under Pharaoh who presided over the entire Egyptian guard.

Now, why does the Scripture tell us exactly whom Joseph was sold to? So that when we look at that detail in light of God's promise for Joseph's future, we will be assured that the steps of a good man are ordered by God (Ps. 37:23). Joseph was being given his next "ordered" step toward the palace!

Do you believe that is true about your life as well? When you experience those multiple attacks, when that friend betrays you, when that person disappoints you and you feel like your world is closing in on you, *God is orchestrating your next step in life.*

Let go and let God. You are too special, too important to God for Him to let you continue on with something that is absolutely nothing. If someone walks out of your life, if you lose a job, if you lose a position or even something worse, don't despair.

Instead say:

> *Lord, I give You thanks because I know You have something greater, something better for me. I know at the end of the day I'm going to laugh again. Others are having their party now, but when their party is over, I'll be the one standing and rejoicing, and no one will be able to change that because my victory and my joy will come from You.*

Like Joseph, your steps are being ordered by God. Even through the pit and the party, you're still on your way to the palace. You ought to throw your hands up and say:

> *Lord, I don't understand; I can't figure things out. But one thing I do know: if You continue to order my steps, then I will get there.*

Born to reign!

No One Can Stop God

Joseph's life is an example for us, to encourage us not to lose heart but to always believe that God will come through and perform His Word on our behalf.

Stay plugged in to the power source. Stay plugged in to the kingdom. Stay plugged in to God. Don't let what you're going through deter you from believing God, praising God, and obeying God.

If the top has been ordained for you, then it is going to happen for you. Let your enemies throw their crazy party. Let them celebrate. Let them think that the pit and their party is a sign that you are finished. Little do they know that destiny is calling you. Listen closely to God when they are having their party, and you will hear greatness calling you onward. Greatness is calling you to keep going and keep believing.

Jesus is your source. He is your strong tower, your deliverer.

As we will see in the chapters that follow, God would be Joseph's strong tower, deliverer, and vindicator; for when God has spoken a thing, He brings it to pass at just the right time. *Remember, that God's timing is just as important as His will; therefore, if it's His will, you still have to wait on His time.* Born to reign!

Chapter Three

THE PRISON

Prison (literal): A place of confinement; a place for the custody of criminals; for the imprisonment of persons convicted of major crimes.

Prison (figurative): A place physical, emotional, or spiritual that corrodes the personality of the prisoner; where self-respect erodes; where long incarceration creates a life apart from free society; where confinement grows first from a restriction or a restraint into a condition of the soul.

Now Joseph was brought down to Egypt, and Potiphar, an officer of Pharaoh, captain of the guard, an Egyptian, bought him from the Ishmaelites who had brought him down there.... Joseph's master took him and put him into the prison, a place where the king's prisoners were confined.
—GENESIS 39:1, 20

IN CHAPTERS 1 and 2, we saw that Joseph's vengeful brothers, fueled by their jealousy and their hatred for

Joseph, threw their brother into a pit, depriving him of food, water, or any comfort whatsoever. So happy were they to be finally ridding themselves of their brother, they proceeded to throw themselves a party to celebrate their freedom and his demise. Nearby, Joseph languished in the pit, suffering the fresh wounds of rejection and abandonment and the nagging discomfort of exposure.

We then watched as Joseph's brazenly cold-hearted brothers had the audacity to sell their youngest sibling to foreign traders—complete strangers, the Ishmaelites. As their name suggests, the Ishmaelites were the descendants of Ishmael, the eldest son of Abraham, born of his concubine, Hagar (see Genesis 16:1-12). These traders were nomadic merchants who frequented Egypt, a wealthy and powerful land, to sell their cargo, human or otherwise. Today we would identify them, in part, as human traffickers. They sold whatever people wanted to buy.

You have a connecting flight to destiny—don't miss it!

It's important for us to understand that it was imperative for Joseph to be in the pit *long enough* so as not to miss the passing Ismaelites. What if he had been able to climb out and free himself without his brothers noticing him? He would have missed his date with destiny.

Joseph had a divine flight to catch. He was on a journey, and God had booked him on a connecting flight to the palace in Egypt. If he yielded to his discomfort and left the waiting area at the gate, he would have missed that flight! But God made sure that Joseph stayed where he was so he could stay on schedule.

In other words, if we grow so uncomfortable with our current situation that we try to get ourselves out of it, then we run the risk of exiting the test prematurely and missing our connecting flight to our next destination in God.

My comrade, be assured that if God has something for you, He'll position you for it. But you must bear with His decisions and His timing until He is finished and ready to move you on.

Surely for Joseph it must have seemed like things were only getting darker. Not only had he suffered rejection and abandonment by his immediate family, he was also now being carried into Egypt—sold into slavery and in bondage to strangers. And it was all because the people he loved hated him because he had their father's favor. Favor may cause you to be hated for no good reason, but favor is worth it!

Can you imagine his trip to Egypt—the tears, the heartache, the stress, the pain? Thinking back to where he had come from, he must have been praying:

> *Lord, You made me some promises, but it seems like I'm going away from them. It seems like my enemies are triumphant over me. They are taking me in the opposite direction from where You promised me I'd go.*

If Joseph only could have known: the darkest hours are just before the dawn.

Are you, like Joseph was, in a dark season now? Maybe you are saying:

> *Lord, You promised me increase, but I'm still experiencing lack. You promised to make my enemies my footstool, but it feels like they are walking all over me. Lord, I'm praising You and*

I'm worshipping You; I'm living to the best of my abilities; but it seems like only the wicked are prospering. It's discouraging.

Be patient. Your flight is about to take off! Be patient.

Today's pit will become tomorrow's palace.

As we will see, an era was coming in Joseph's life when the enemy couldn't stop him no matter how much he tried. The same will be true for you. You need to stir up your faith, encourage yourself, and tell yourself: "I may look rough around the edges. I may even look raggedy right now—I might have some holes here and there. But even if I look a mess right now, God made me some promises, and He is watching over His Word to bring it to pass."

None of us fully understand the providence of God, and this was especially true of Joseph's brothers. They had no clue that, according to the providence of God, it was very important that Joseph was held in the pit. It was necessary so that he would end up in Egypt.

The providence of God means that God is in full control of all things at all times. Even when it seems like God is absent, He is there: "Behold, He who guards Israel shall neither slumber nor sleep" (Ps. 121:4).

Hebrews 1:3 says that God "upholds all things by the word of His power." That means, unless God permits: The sun can't deviate from rising and setting. The moon can't diverge from its assignment. The seas cannot move beyond their boundaries. Everything in the universe must obey God in the way He commands it to. He is in full control at all times.

So while Joseph's clueless brothers rejoiced over what they believed would be the end of their brother, God was

The Prison

getting Joseph ready for greatness. How short-sighted and foolish their judgment was. They would have been wise to treat Joseph with respect and dignity. For the person who is in the pit today may be in the palace tomorrow.

As they would soon enough find out.

Prospering in the House of Bondage

> The Lord was with Joseph, so that he became a prosperous man. He was in the house of his master, the Egyptian. His master saw that the Lord was with him and that the Lord made all that he did to prosper.
> —Genesis 39:2–3

So the Ishmaelites took Joseph bound down to Egypt. There he was sold into slavery by his human traffickers. He had made the first of several important transitions in his destiny. This first one was to be changed from the most highly favored son of his father to a virtual orphan and the property of a foreign stranger.

Does that sound like the pathway to greatness that the Most High would ever require of one of His sons or daughters? How much more contradictory to the promise of God could you get? Hadn't God supernaturally revealed to Joseph that the sun, the moon, and the eleven stars—representing his father, his mother, and his brothers—were going to bow to him? But he was a slave instead. Freedom was dead for him. Family was dead for him. His future as a man of promise and prosperity was dead for him (or seemed like it was). How unlikely do you think it must have seemed to him that he would ever inherit what God had promised him?

Here's the key: No matter how bad things look, no matter

how much things seem to be defying God's promise to you, don't give up. God knows exactly what He is doing.

- Don't give up because you are experiencing hard times.

- Don't give up because folks are mishandling you.

- Don't give up because people have walked out of your life, especially when you needed them most.

- Don't give up because you cannot understand the season that you're in. Remember it's a cost to be the boss!

Don't you give up on God, but know for certain that God is working all things together for your good: "We know that all things work together for good to those who love God, to those who are called according to His purpose" (Rom. 8:28).

If by the grace of God we live long enough, we all will discover that when God has favored and handpicked you, there is nothing the devil can do about it. You are in the position you're in today because of destiny; and the good news is, nothing can happen to you that God doesn't allow to happen. The Bible declares "no weapon that is formed against you shall prosper" (Isa. 54:17).

It won't matter if your difficulties involve people of power and influence. Those were the kind of people Joseph faced. It won't matter if, compared with them, you seem to have or be nothing or you feel that you aren't even in their league. Joseph was a rural teenager being processed by God for greatness. The enormous gap in experience and status didn't matter in Joseph's situation. And it won't matter in yours, because when you are born to reign you can't be stopped.

Verse 2 says that Joseph was "a prosperous man." How can that be since he was a slave? Since when are slaves "prosperous"? The difference in his case was this: *He was prosperous because God's hand of favor was on him.*

No matter where you go, divine favor is like a shadow following your every step. Regardless of how people oppose you or try to limit you, favor will always get you through and continue to shine on you. King David said:

> Why do the nations rage, and the peoples plot in vain? The kings of the earth set themselves, and the rulers take counsel together, against the Lord and against His anointed, saying, "Let us tear off their bonds and cast away their ropes from us." He who sits in the heavens laughs; the Lord ridicules them.
> —Psalm 2:1–4

God will ensure you have the last laugh. He will embarrass those who oppose His chosen people.

Isaiah also writes: "It is He who sits upon the circle of the earth, and the inhabitants are as grasshoppers, who stretches out the heavens as a curtain, and spreads them out as a tent to dwell in" (40:22). In other words, if God has to turn the universe around to bless you, He will. You are that special to Him.

Remember, divine providence states that God is in full control—all the time. He is meticulously moving things into position for the fulfillment of His will and for His glory. It was mandatory that Joseph got to Egypt, even if his own brothers had to sell him as a slave to get him there.

And God proved His divine providence in Joseph's life because even when Joseph was sold to Potiphar, the Lord was with him and blessed him (Gen. 39:3). As the captain of the Egyptian guard, Potiphar had a big job—to protect Pharaoh. He would have been similar to the head of the Secret Service, sworn to protect the president of the United States. He was the chief bodyguard for Pharaoh and commanded a legion of lesser ranking guards.

He probably was also the head of the state police. They formed part of the Egyptian army but were also largely employed in civil duties that could have included executions. Though we don't know the extent of his powers, Potiphar possibly could have held the power of life and death in his hand.

There's no doubt, however, that he was a man of great authority and great means. His residence was probably close to the royal court, and he would have been rewarded handsomely for keeping Pharaoh safe and secure.

And Joseph was now this man's slave; which meant that even though Joseph shared in the well-to-do status of Potiphar's house, he was nevertheless living in a house of bondage—yet *prospering*!

"The Lord was with Joseph" (v. 2). He was prospering even in the house of bondage because *God was with him*. And his master could see it. He noticed God was blessing Joseph and that everything he put his hand to turned out well.

From slave to overseer

> Joseph found favor in his sight and served him. So he made him overseer over his house, and all that he had he put under his charge. From the time that

The Prison

> he had made him overseer in his house and over all that he had, the LORD blessed the Egyptian's house on account of Joseph. So the blessing of the LORD was on all that he had in the house and in the field.
> —GENESIS 39:4–5

Imagine that! Joseph entered Potiphar's house as a slave and now he is the *overseer* of his house. Potiphar had enough sense to know God's favor was on Joseph and that he shouldn't disturb it. He probably thought: "I'm not going to handle this boy like his family did. I'd be foolish to because he has so much favor upon him! My house is blessed because of him."

Isn't it amazing that strangers will appreciate you more than the people who know you best? Jesus noted this when He said, "A prophet is not without honor, except in his own country, and among his own relatives, and in his own house" (Mark 6:4).

Potiphar gave Joseph control over everything he had: his bank account, his stocks, his land, his crops, his livestock—everything. That's divine intervention! *Divine intervention* simply means "when God steps in."

Have you ever watched tag-team wrestling? Think of it like that—tag Jesus in! Let Him handle those big wrestlers. Let Him fight your battles. When He intervenes, you win the fight!

The divine intervention in Joseph's life also shows us that wherever favored individuals go, they will shine. Their "coat" might be stripped away and discarded by man, but the favor that the coat represented was given by God. They took the coat away from Joseph, but they could not touch the favor. God gave him another coat—as estate overseer of the captain of the guard for all of Egypt! This was a new symbol of authority, favor, and distinction for Joseph. This coat represented only one of the colors of the coat of many colors that Joseph wore. Joseph had many more coats to wear, and so do you!

Wherever God puts you, you're going to expand, you're going to mature, you're going to prosper; and people won't be able to deny the magnitude of the favor of God on your life. Maybe God will have you take the stairs to the top instead of the elevator. By the time you finish your climb you might be sweaty and tired, but there is going to be a new "coat" for you to wear when you get there. There is going to be a new mantle of favor and authority for you to wear.

You could say that's what happened with Joseph—it was a tough climb from the pit to Egyptian high society. It was no relaxing elevator ride. But as he walked those "stairs," his owner, Potiphar, had sense enough to see what he had in Joseph. And he gave Joseph authority over everything. What a miracle: from slave to overseer!

Nothing but favor

> So he left all that he had in Joseph's charge, and he had no concerns regarding anything except the food he ate.
> —Genesis 39:6

The trust Potiphar had for Joseph only grew. God blesses those He can trust with other people's things. (The opposite is also true: He doesn't bless those He cannot trust with other people's things.)

Joseph's favor grew along with Potiphar's trust. It expanded to the point that Potiphar left all of his money in Joseph's care and didn't even require an accounting of it! He did not pay attention to any of his riches or possessions. He took no concern for them because he trusted Joseph that much to handle everything with integrity. The only thing he owned that he took notice of were the meals Joseph had the servants prepare for him. They must have been so good that he looked forward to every one of them!

These verses show us that Joseph was receiving preferential treatment. He was favored! He was helping Potiphar become rich by managing his affairs carefully, responsibly, and with integrity. Everything Joseph put his hand to multiplied in a favorable way. Joseph had not forgotten that although he was an overseer with great responsibility he was also still a slave. But he knew that if God blessed Potiphar, then he would be next. So keep doing what you're doing; you're next!

When you are favored, whatever you touch is going to be approved. It is going to be blessed; it is going to increase; it is going to be multiplied. Whatever is touched by someone who is favored by God will yield favorable results.

What a time of refreshing it must have been in Joseph's life. His season of suffering had finally changed to a time of blessing and favor. Perhaps his hour of pain and sorrow had actually come to an end. The rejection, abandonment, betrayal, and loss he had suffered at the hands of his brothers were fading into the past. He now lived a new life in a new world where God was blessing him in ways even he recognized as incredible and miraculous. At last, instead of a heavy sigh on his heart, he had a new song on his lips.

That would soon change. Joseph's destiny was calling once again.

Things Heat Up

The temptress

> Now Joseph was handsome and well-built. After a time, his master's wife took notice of Joseph and said, "Lie with me." But he refused and said to his master's wife, "My master does not concern himself with anything concerning me in the house, and he has committed all that he has to my charge. There is none greater in this house than I. He has kept nothing back from me but you, because you are his wife. How then can I do this great wickedness and sin against God?" She spoke to Joseph every day, but he did not listen to her about lying with her or being with her.
> —Genesis 39:6–10

The devil always shows up to try to dispossess you and take you out of position. He comes with one intention: to ruin the good work God has started.

But Joseph recognized what was going on. He knew this woman's advances not only threatened everything he had but, more importantly, also jeopardized his communion and fellowship with God. His mind raced as he quickly summed up what was happening: "I am responsible for all this man's money, all his clothing, all his uniforms; I make sure everything in his entire house is in order. He's made me an overseer of his entire personal life. He's given me everything in his household to run—except her. This woman is trying to destroy what I have now and what I'm going to have in the future. I've come too far from that terrible day in the pit. There's no way I'm going to let this temptress from hell stop me from coming into what God promised me."

You get into trouble when you start crossing boundaries or lines you have no business going over. Trouble multiplies when you don't or won't wait on God. Out of impatience, you put your hands on something that you think will make things better. But it is going to destroy you whether you recognize it or not. You must guard your future!

Joseph was mature enough to see that. And he would have none of it.

He said to this woman, "As good as you look, do me a favor and deal me out. If I take what you're offering, then I would lose what God has offered."

Notice in verse 10 that she kept after him. This wasn't a onetime seduction. She was hammering away at him, trying to get him to break. Doesn't that sound just like temptation? Just like the way our flesh works on us? But each time when she drew near to seduce him, Joseph flatly denied her. "No deal!" he said.

Think about something that you need to refuse. Refuse it! Tell the enemy, "I'm not going to jeopardize what God is doing in my life." Joseph was not willing to jeopardize his paradise by allowing his flesh to dictate to his future.

Invitation to secret sin

> But it happened one day that Joseph went into the house to do his work, and none of the men of the house was there. She caught him by his clothing, saying, "Lie with me." But he left his clothing in her hand and fled and got outside.
> —Genesis 39:11–12

What would you do if you could do anything you wanted to, knowing that nobody would ever see it, hear about it, or learn about it? Would you still choose to do the right thing? How you answer that is the difference between the person who lives by integrity and the person who doesn't.

Joseph was all alone in Potiphar's house. His master had a great responsibility—to safeguard Pharaoh and all those in his palace. He probably worked long hours and was away from home for stretches of time. All the other men and servants were gone. He was alone in the home with His master's wife.

Maybe the wife felt neglected. Maybe she was an adulteress and Joseph wasn't her first victim. Regardless of her reason, now she was inviting him to secretly enjoy her.

He was being offered the perfect opportunity to yield to his flesh and satisfy his youthful desire. Perhaps she would even be willing to make it an ongoing secret affair—a clandestine (undercover) way for him to have his youthful needs met. It was a tempting offer for a young man in the prime of his life.

And who would ever know? Who would ever see? It was just the two of them. He could have yielded and they could have had their way with each other and nobody would have been the wiser.

Except for God.

Joseph knew that what he did in secret wasn't a secret to God. He knew he would be sinning against God and there would be consequences upon the plans God had for him. He knew the devil had placed this adulteress in his path to ruin him and put an end to his future in God. Joseph had a heart of integrity. So he refused her.

It was risky, though. He was a slave. She had authority

over him. How might she retaliate to a slave spurning her advances? Joseph was vulnerable because he had no defense against her except his integrity. But the alternative was unthinkable to him.

In the same way, even if you become vulnerable, even if you feel like you're in a state in which you can't help yourself, still tell the devil no. Maintain your innocence before God, fully assured that when God has a plan for you, even the worst that could happen to you is a part of His bigger plan.

Why had the devil suddenly come? Why now? Why had he shown up out of the blue and placed this temptation before Joseph? What was the devil really after in Joseph? The same thing he was after when Joseph first had his dreams, when he was the favored son of Jacob. He wanted to strip Joseph of his "coat."

He wanted to ruin Joseph's life, his calling, his destiny. He wanted to destroy Joseph's place of authority in Egypt and banish him to a life in chains or, better yet, have him executed for offending Potiphar and his wife. Either way, he was out to bury Joseph's future.

The accuser and the lie

> She spoke to him using these words, saying, "The Hebrew servant, whom you have brought to us, came in to me to mock me. When I lifted up my voice and cried out, he left his clothing with me and fled outside."
> —GENESIS 39:17–18

It is a well-known fact that a lobster shed it shells numerous of times. It must shed so it can form a new, stronger, more protective shell that will enable it to grow to the next stage in its life. But shedding its shell means that for a time the young lobster is wholly vulnerable to predators in the sea.

Now, those young lobsters would not be living according to God's design for them if they somehow could refuse to shed their first protective shell. In fact, they'd die. Even with lowly marine life, you have to shed a coat every now and then if God wants to take you higher.

Similarly, Joseph had a protective covering of favor and authority that kept him safe within the halls of Potiphar's house. It helped to secure and maintain the high position he held and enabled him to do his part for the Egyptian government.

But God's time had come for Joseph, and the Lord needed that protective "shell" to be shed so He could cover Joseph with a new, stronger shell that would sustain him at the next level. To strip Joseph of his protective covering, God allowed a false accuser to rise up against him whose lie would send him to prison. No matter what comes your way, remember: it did not come to stay; just sit back and let God have His way.

Again, God spared his life, just as He did when Joseph's brothers thought to kill him. In this case, Potiphar, as head of the Egyptian state security forces, would easily have had the authority to put one slave to death at his own discretion. Especially one who was alleged to have made an attempt to rape his wife! But because of destiny and God's favor on Joseph, Potiphar chose to send him to prison instead of execute him. Remember, God's got this! Just be still because your prison has a purpose. Who could have told Joseph that the prison was his entrance to the palace?

Understand this, however: God's purpose in shedding

Joseph's covering was *wholly redemptive.* Yes, Joseph would become completely vulnerable as an inmate. Potiphar's protective shell would be gone. But God would protect him. In the meantime, He would use the imprisonment to fit Joseph with a new, protective coating of greater authority that would lift him up to the highest level in Pharaoh's kingdom besides the throne itself.

Miraculously, he would rise in authority even above Potiphar. Born to reign!

DESTINY CALLS AGAIN

From overseer to inmate

> When his master heard the words of his wife, which she spoke to him, saying, "This is what your servant did to me," he became enraged. Joseph's master took him and put him into the prison, a place where the king's prisoners were confined.
> —GENESIS 39:19–20

For a second time, what Joseph thought was evil triumphing over him was actually the plan of God moving him closer to his destiny. He was experiencing his second great transition towards God's destiny for his life. He was on God's providential schedule, and it required that he must be imprisoned. He would have to endure the prison before he reached the palace. Just like Joseph, you and I have to endure our prison experiences before we reach the palace.

But, remember, Joseph was known as a trustworthy person and was well-favored. He was no criminal. In fact, he was anything but a criminal. He had no record of wrongdoing and, in fact, had a reputation of being just the opposite of a criminal.

So how was he going to be thrown into the dungeons of Egypt—where God needed him to go—if someone didn't accuse him? Thus, it was according to God's providential plan that Joseph was the victim of a liar, that he was falsely accused, that he was condemned unjustly.

And because he was a slave, he had no rights. It was nothing for Potiphar to send him straight to prison without a trial. Again, Potiphar could have executed him; he had the authority. But he didn't have the power because it was not God's will for Joseph. Your enemies do not have the power to execute you, but God will use them to process you. Stay the course, and you will be the boss!

Notice that Joseph was not allowed even to speak in his own defense. Doesn't that seem surprising, considering how trustworthy Potiphar considered Joseph to be? Does it make sense that this man who trusted Joseph with everything he owned wouldn't even give him the opportunity to defend himself? (And tell his master that his wife was a liar!)

But it wasn't in God's plan. Joseph was offered no such opportunity to defend himself because God wanted him in prison! The way to the palace was through the prison. He was born to reign!

Raised up in lockdown

> But the LORD was with Joseph and showed him mercy and gave him favor in the sight of the keeper of the prison. The keeper of the prison committed all the prisoners that were in the prison to the charge of Joseph. So whatever they did there, he was the one responsible for it. The keeper of the prison did

The Prison

not concern himself with anything that was under Joseph's charge because the LORD was with him. And whatever he did, the LORD made it to prosper.
—GENESIS 39:21–23

Now, when you go to prison, aren't you're supposed to be in lockdown? Aren't you supposed to be locked in a cell, doing only what you're ordered to do? Aren't you supposed to be stripped of your freedoms and live and move and have your being as the state dictates?

Not Joseph. God had a plan for Joseph while he was in prison that would astound everyone. It would bring Joseph to Pharaoh's attention. It would exalt him to Pharaoh's right hand. It would confirm and fulfill the dreams God had given him. *God graced him in prison with the same favor he had in Potiphar's house!*

Joseph was so saturated with favor that when the warden saw the favor of God on him, he sat back and told him, "Stand up and take charge of things for me!" Even that jailer had the sense to know Joseph's favor was unlike any he'd ever seen before. When God places favor on you, you're unstoppable!

Joseph was put in charge of all the prisoners and all of their assigned duties. And he did it so well and with so much integrity that the warden didn't even bother to oversee Joseph's decisions. He essentially let him run the place. Doesn't that sound exactly like the kind of favor Joseph enjoyed when he was a slave in Potiphar's house?

He had been a slave and now he was a prisoner, yet neither position could stop God's favor from saturating his life. And by the way, favor demands attention!

You may be in a prison, but you're heading to the palace.

Just don't allow your *now* cause you give up on your *later*! Joseph didn't.

Next stop, Pharaoh's palace.

Chapter Four

THE PALACE

Palace (literal): A large and stately house; as the official residence of a sovereign or exalted personage.

Palace (figurative): An ascended state in life where great wealth and authority are centered and where serenity and power coexist; a high place of prominence, abundance, glory, and nobility.

The cupbearer of the king of Egypt and his baker offended their lord, the king of Egypt. Pharaoh was angry with his two officials.... So he put them...in the prison, the place where Joseph was confined...and he attended to them.... Then the cupbearer and the baker both had a dream the same night, each man with his own dream and each dream with its own interpretation.
—Genesis 40:1–5

So Pharaoh sent and called for Joseph, and they brought him hastily out of the dungeon. Pharaoh said to Joseph, "I have dreamed a dream, and there is no one who can interpret it. I have heard it said of you that you can understand a dream to interpret it." Joseph answered Pharaoh, saying, "It is not in me. God will give Pharaoh a favorable answer."

—Genesis 41:14–16

And Pharaoh said to Joseph, "Since God has shown you all this...you will be over my house, and according to your word all my people will be ruled....See, I have set you over all the land of Egypt." Pharaoh took off his ring from his hand and put it on Joseph's hand and arrayed him in clothes of fine linen and put a gold chain around his neck....So he set him over all the land of Egypt.

—Genesis 41:39–43

We have seen in the previous chapters that Joseph dreamed two dreams, both of them revealing how he would one day reign over his brothers and his father and mother. When he told his first dream to his brothers, they envied him. When he told them his second dream, they hated him.

Reviling him secretly, they mocked him and called him a "dreamer." They plotted against him until an opportunity presented itself, then stripped him of his coat of many colors that Jacob his father made for him, threw him into a wild game pit in the wilderness, and had a party. Then they sold him to the Ishmaelites, a band of nomadic merchantmen who passed by on their way to Egypt in search of goods, money, and profits. The Ishmaelites took Joseph into Egypt and sold him as a slave to Potiphar, the captain of the national Egyptian guard.

We saw because of the great favor and abilities God bestowed on Joseph that Potiphar placed the slave in charge of his entire house. God blessed everything Joseph touched. Everything he put his hand to increased to Potiphar's advantage.

We learned that there is something about an individual who is covered by the favor of God. No matter what their circumstance in life, they always shine. No matter how badly they are mistreated—should they be opposed, misrepresented, or mishandled, they always receive the good God intends for them to have.

So it was with Joseph. We saw that the more he oversaw Potiphar's estate, the more Potiphar prospered. He caused his master's house to bloom and revel in bountiful growth. We watched this prosperity continue its upward rise until the day the devil showed up to ruin Joseph.

The same accuser who brazenly intruded into the pure and holy serenity of the Garden of Eden to thwart Adam and Eve also came into the exalted courts of Egypt to stop a favored child of God from glorifying the Lord. Satan knows he cannot stop God. So, rather than pursue futility, he goes against the weaker opponent—humanity. He does everything in his power to stop us or move us out of our God-given position.

We saw that Potiphar's wife became the devil's instrument with which to tempt Joseph to sin, fail, and fall. She lusted for the slave and openly offered herself to him. Joseph's heart beat with personal integrity and the fear of God. He refused the temptress, telling her that Potiphar had given him the job of overseeing everything in his house—except her. My friend, if you're going to be successful, then you must know when to say no.

But we saw that the devil was persistent. She wouldn't let up. She came back to Joseph day after day but was refused. One day, Joseph actually had to flee for the sake of his future. As he did, she grabbed his garment and pulled it off. It became false evidence that she used to accuse him of attempted rape. Spurned and embarrassed by Joseph, she sought revenge. She falsely accused him to Potiphar. It was a major crime.

We saw that Joseph had done all he could to honor his master, fear God, and keep his heart and actions blameless before both of them. Now, from no fault of his own, he had been thrown into a fight he could not win—he was falsely accused by one of Egypt's first ladies. He was in an impossible predicament. Potiphar was a powerful, high-ranking government and military official. Joseph was a slave with no legal rights. How could Joseph escape his master's clutches?

Only God could save him.

Stay in the Fight

What do you do when you find yourself in a fight you just can't win? It's not that you're a novice in battle. You even think of yourself as a warrior. You've won battles before. You know the weapons of your warfare are spiritual, not carnal. You know how to pray, you know how to fast, and you know how to praise God. But this time, it feels like you are being conquered. This time, you are in an uncommon battle. It feels like you are in the fight of your life—and losing. Why? What's happening?

Remember that "the steps of a good man are ordered by the Lord" (Ps. 37:23, kjv). Did you catch that? A good man's steps are ordered "by the Lord." If God is ordering your steps as He did Joseph's, then what you are going through is *part of the plan. The fire is designed for your refinement.*

Why? Because God will test everyone He blesses. Those who endure the test before they are blessed will have a spiritual résumé. They will be able to tell others about the fire (the pit, the party, and the prison) they have gone through—the fire they endured even after God made great and glorious promises to them—and how God brought them through their testing. Stay in the fight!

Now, the fire had to have been difficult for Joseph because he was innocent. He was in a hard place because of what someone else said about him. He knew he was in a strange place, falsely accused, and should not have been where he was. But he trusted that God was with him. He did not understand the *why* behind the pit, the party, and the prison; but God knew just what to do to build Joseph's character.

You're probably saying: "I didn't know it was going to be *this* hard. I thought after I received the promise I would be on my way to the palace. I thought a limo was coming to get me."

(Wow, I thought so too; but to my surprise I was picked up by a war tank, not a limo!)

You're seeing it your way. But the Bible says, "Trust in the Lord with all your heart, and lean not on your own understanding; in all your ways acknowledge Him, and He will direct your paths" (Prov. 3:5–6).

Joseph's promise was that he would reign over his brothers. They would make obeisance to him. Instead, Joseph had been held captive in a pit, sold into slavery, accused of a major crime by a high-ranking liar, and sentenced indefinitely to prison for a crime he didn't commit. Did you notice that none of *those* details were included in his prophetic dreams? But the injustices didn't mean God's promise had changed—the prophetic dreams still belonged only to Joseph; the palace was still his. Knowing He would need to refine Joseph's heart and teach him to live by faith, God did not tell Joseph that he would live behind bars first. Just like He did not tell us that the process would come first, then the promise.

Stay in the fight—and remember that greatness is not for the faithless. God requires faith from us:

> For in it the righteousness of God is revealed from faith to faith. As it is written, "The just shall live by faith."
> —Romans 1:17

> And without faith it is impossible to please God, for he who comes to God must believe that He exists and that He is a rewarder of those who diligently seek Him.
> —Hebrews 11:6

And Joseph, like us, had to fight to keep faith alive in his heart, to keep believing God was with him, to keep believing God was for him, to keep believing He would see the manifestation of what God had promised him.

> Fight the good fight of faith.
> —1 Timothy 6:12

> I believe I will see the goodness of the Lord in the land of the living.
> —Psalm 27:13

The reason your preparation, your process, is so long and so intense is because of what He has for you in the end. Some of you are saying: "It's been ten years! I feel like throwing in the towel," or, "Nothing has happened yet." Well, who told you it was going to happen overnight? Who told you it was going to happen without a process? Certainly it wasn't God, because He processes us before He blesses us. Joseph was seventeen when he got his word, but it took thirteen years before he got the promise.

Stay in the fight; and remember that before God places your promise in your hands, He is going to make sure you can hold it.

When God Is Through, There's More Favor for You

If the same process is occurring in your life that happened in Joseph's life, then keep believing that the palace is yours, the favor is yours; even if for now you are in a pit or having a prison experience.

Maybe God is not explaining any of the details to you either. As far as you are concerned, it feels like your life is finished. None of it seems to line up with the word God has given you.

But there is something about the word of God over your life: it will never return to God void. When God is taking you somewhere you've never been before, the path obviously will be unfamiliar to you. But remember that God has been there before.

Would you have imagined that God was taking Joseph into a foreign land to make him great? Probably not. And I wouldn't have either, but that's what He did; so be still wherever He positions you. He has the power to give you favor and elevate you.

During your journey to the palace, God may allow folks to "ride" over your head. To the psalmist, that fact was no surprise. Psalm 66:12 says, "You have allowed people to ride over our heads." He may even allow you to experience things that would drive other people out of their minds. But He knows what He is doing; He knows how much you can bear. The best part is, when He is through, there's more favor for you!

God is not threatened by things like pits and prisons. He's so much bigger. His grace is sufficient; His strength is made perfect when you're weak, and His plans will always stand (2 Cor. 12:9; Isa. 46:9–10). Favor like a shadow will follow you, like it did Joseph, wherever you go!

What kind of pit or prison are you facing? Are people trying to bite and devour you? Maybe your finances are on hold, your marriage is in trouble, or it seems like everything in your life is getting worse, not better.

Know for certain that whatever you are going through is only temporary. God is just molding and shaping you so that you can master your new season, the palace. You might not understand it, but don't resist it. He is the master Potter. We are but His clay:

> Shall the clay say to the potter, "What are you making?"
> —Isaiah 45:9

The Palace

While God is operating on you, stop asking Him:

Why are You cutting me here? Why are You cutting me there? You could have done it this way or even that way. Why did You allow this person to do what they did to me? Why am I struggling? You promised me such great things and showed me such wonderful dreams, but it seems like nothing is happening for me.

Instead, close your eyes and tell God,

I am going to sleep, and when I wake up You'll have it worked out.

Remember, everyone God raises up to reign will be "experienced." They will have a spiritual résumé. In Joseph's case, his résumé stated that his own family members sold him into slavery! That's a tough way to get your "experience" and to have your character tested and molded.

We saw that the favor of God was so heavy on Joseph's life that even as a prisoner he was put in charge of the prison. That's incredible! How do you take over the prison when you are a prisoner? How does that happen? The favor of God. Favor, like a shadow, will follow you wherever you go!

To the Egyptians, Joseph was an unusual slave. He was a Hebrew. Out of all the prisoners, they noticed him. What they saw in him that they couldn't fully understand was the anointing of God on his life. To God, Joseph was the governor—the man in charge. It was simply that God had put him in prison to train him for his high position. God uses the foolish things of the world to confound the wise:

> But God has chosen the foolish things of the world to confound the wise. God has chosen the weak things of the world to confound the things which are mighty.
> —1 CORINTHIANS 1:27

There is nothing the enemy can do with someone who is blessed and highly favored by God. It doesn't matter where you go; the favor of God is greater than your location or situation. God's favor will put you in charge regardless of where you are or who you are. And that frightens the enemy.

In Joseph's case, the prison warden recognized (just as Potiphar had) the amazing and rare anointing on Joseph. Instinctively he knew Joseph could handle anything, so he appointed him to run the prison and manage his affairs! Remember that the anointing God gives supersedes the works of man. *When God is through, there's more favor for you.*

LET GO AND LET GOD

> Pharaoh was angry with his two officials…so he put them…in the prison, the place where Joseph was confined…and he attended to them. Then the cupbearer and the baker…both had a dream the same night.
> —GENESIS 40:2–3, 5

Our brother Joseph is in prison, where he should've been treated like every other inmate; but instead he has been given the keys to kingdom. I believe he actually was entrusted with the *literal* keys to the prison. How else would he have been able to perform his duties for the warden if he didn't have access to all areas of the prison?

In fact, I believe Joseph could have let himself right out the back door and disappeared into the Egyptian wilderness! He had the run of the facility. He could have taken his time and planned his escape, made sure he had enough supplies to survive his trek to freedom. He could have become the subject of the biggest jail break in Egyptian history! I believe he literally had the power to free himself from the slavery and bondage he was experiencing. So why didn't he? What kept him from running?

If Joseph had gotten caught up in trying to change his environment, then he never would have seen God's plan go into action. If he had changed his focus to trying to relieve his difficult situation, then it would have been the first clue to us as readers that he did not recognize the hand of God working mightily on his behalf.

But he didn't run—and I believe it's because he knew God was working out His plan in his life and that he had to wait until God was finished.

Let go and let God!

There is something about when God brings you into a place in life where a refining process must take place: you can't get away from it. Even if you were to try to escape it, you'd fail because it is not in you to run. The call of God is too strong. The Bible says deep calls to deep—the heart of God calls to the heart of man, and man freezes in holy obedience; he won't move, even when being severely tested.

David wrote about this. He remained still while God dealt with him:

> Deep calls to deep...all Your waves and billows passed over me.
> —Psalm 42:7

Something deep inside tells you: "You must stay right where He has put you. Even though it is painful, there is a glory coming out of this. Yes, you are struggling. Yes, you could run through the back door and escape this. But greatness is telling you, 'Don't move.'"

Pray and determine that you will not allow anything into your life that could cause you to abort the process and lose everything God has for you. You don't want to have to go back and start all over again. Keep reminding yourself: "I was born to reign. I might be in a prison at the moment, but it's just a stopover before the palace." Let your attitude be,

> *Lord, Your will be done, not mine.*

Don't try to hurry God:

> But let patience perfect its work, that you may be perfect and complete, lacking nothing.
> —JAMES 1:4

It is important to develop patience. Patience will keep you out of the unnecessary problems that result when you try to get what God isn't ready for you to have.

Let go and let God!

SUDDENLY!

For Joseph, there was no visible way he could get out of that house of bondage—unless he were to make a run for it. He had been sentenced to prison indefinitely by one of the highest officials in the world.

Nobody was going to let him out without an order from the very top of the Egyptian national government. He had no public defender. He had no court of appeals. He had no supporters outside the prison walls calling for his release. Nobody was holding press conferences for him. He had no spokesperson standing up for his cause. He had no magistrate who was willing to hear his case. Egyptian society didn't work like that. Short of an outright miracle, he was going to sit in prison until the day he died.

Thank God Joseph served the God of miracles. He says:

> See, I will do a new thing, now it shall spring forth; shall you not be aware of it? I will even make a way in the wilderness, and rivers in the desert.
> —Isaiah 43:19

"*Now* it shall spring forth," it says (emphasis added). *Now* means "right now"—*suddenly*!

God was about to do something suddenly that would take Joseph straight to the palace. He was about to pave a new lane on the road Joseph was traveling to reach his destiny. Here's what happened:

- *Suddenly* Pharaoh's chief butler and baker landed in the prison one morning.

- *Suddenly* Joseph was in the presence of two men who only the day before were living and working in the presence of Pharaoh.

- *Suddenly* Joseph had a connection to the very top authority of the Egyptian government—by no planning, strategizing, or cunning of his own. No press secretary, liaison, or committee had done this on Joseph's behalf.

- *Suddenly* God Himself had hand delivered the two men right into his situation.

You simply cannot figure out God's ways. When He's ready to move, He's ready to move—there is no way you can predict when or how He is going to get you out of the situation you are in.

> For My thoughts are not your thoughts, nor are your ways My ways, says the LORD. For as the heavens are higher than the earth, so are My ways higher than your ways, and My thoughts than your thoughts.
> —ISAIAH 55:8–9

Joseph couldn't see it, but God had been behind the scenes meticulously putting the necessary things into place that would get Joseph to the palace. Once God's time comes: *boom, it's done! Suddenly.*

God patiently waits for the *kairos* moment—His perfect time—to move you into your promise.

The Butler and the Baker

> Then the cupbearer and the baker for the king of Egypt, who were confined in the prison, both had a dream the same night.
> —GENESIS 40:5

Because Joseph had been put in charge of the other prisoners, the captain of the prison guard told him to watch over the two new prisoners. Joseph now was responsible for these royal servants—the cupbearer, or butler, and the baker—who had come straight from Pharaoh's presence. Do you see the connection God was setting up? Joseph now had in his charge two men who had a direct line to

The Palace

Pharaoh himself. Pharaoh was deciding what to do with these two servants while he let them sweat out their fate in prison. Eventually they were going to hear from the king again, and Joseph knew that. God had made a strategic move on Joseph's behalf by putting him in touch with these two prisoners.

And then—*suddenly*—here come the prophetic dreams again. Of course, dreams are something Joseph is quite familiar with! By that time, in fact, Joseph should have been wary of prophetic dreams. They were what had gotten him into trouble in the first place! You could say he was where he was because of prophetic dreams.

So we see that the butler and the baker each dreamed a dream on the same night. The next morning, both of them were extremely distressed by what they had dreamed. Joseph instantly noticed the down-and-out look they wore and asked these servants of Pharaoh, "Why are you so sad?" (see Genesis 40:6–7).

What an unusual question. Prison isn't a happy place for *anyone*. It's not as if Joseph should have been surprised to see that these two new arrivals had long faces. After all, just the day before they had been serving in Pharaoh's presence, but now they are in jail waiting for him to decide what he would do with them. He might decide to execute them. Their very lives were in his hands. Why would Joseph even expect them to be in a normal, pleasant mood?

These guys must have looked worse than anybody else in the jail—even worse than what was usual for new prisoners. They looked bad enough for Joseph to stop what he was doing and ask them what their problem was.

In addition, if anyone in that prison had a reason to be sad, it was *Joseph*. He had been imprisoned after being falsely accused; he had been scarred by his brothers; he had been set up and betrayed by Potiphar's wife, whom he had faithfully served when he was in their house; and he knew he was going to be in prison for the rest of his life. But he was worrying instead about someone else's distress.

What do these things tell us about Joseph? That He was more concerned about glorifying God than about his own immediate happiness. When God's anointing and favor is on you, you will be concerned more about others even while you are experiencing hard times.

Joseph was so concerned, he asked them, *"What in the world is happening with you guys?"* The Bible says that both of them then told Joseph their dreams. And Joseph answered them with encouragement—He said: "God is an interpreter of dreams" (see Genesis 40:8).

This is an amazing answer for several reasons:

1. Genesis 40:12 and 18 tell us that *Joseph* interpreted their dreams. Back in Genesis 37 Joseph had two dreams but had no interpretation for them. He couldn't figure them out. Now, in prison, God is giving *him* the revelation for other people's dreams. God had matured Joseph during his ordeal from a dreamer to a dream interpreter. And because of that maturity, Joseph soon would interpret a dream for Pharaoh that would catapult him into the fulfillment of his calling in God.

2. God always uses things that man least expects, things that man would not notice. He uses what looks small to man but is actually big.

Man misjudges its importance. In this case, dreams had put Joseph in the pit. How fitting that God would use dreams to get him out of prison! How awesome are God's ways. Dreams would reverse the very situation that dreams had gotten Joseph into!

3. Joseph answered their problem with a solution. In other words, he was a problem-solver. He was being prepared by God with an anointing that would solve the problems of others. He soon would be solving much, much bigger problems that affected the entire nation of Egypt.

When Joseph shared his revelations with them, he told the chief butler: "Within three days Pharaoh will lift up your head and restore you to your place, and you will deliver Pharaoh's cup into his hand in the same way you did before when you were his cupbearer" (v. 13).

Then he said to the baker, "Within three days Pharaoh will lift your head from off you and will hang you on a tree, and the birds will eat your flesh from you" (v. 19).

Both dreams came to pass: "[Pharaoh] restored the chief cupbearer to his position again, and he put the cup into Pharaoh's hand. However, he hanged the chief baker, just as Joseph had interpreted to them" (Gen. 40:21–22).

"My Ticket Out of Here!"

"But remember me when it is well with you, and show kindness, I pray you, to me, and make mention of me to Pharaoh, and get me out of this house. For I was indeed kidnapped out of the land of the

> Hebrews, and I have done nothing that they should put me in the dungeon."...Yet, the chief cupbearer did not remember Joseph, but forgot him.
> —GENESIS 40:14–15, 23

How often we misinterpret a situation, a relationship, or a circumstance we think is a sign that our difficult season is coming to an end. Then, when things don't happen like we think they're going to, discouragement sets in. Victory doesn't come until our faith shifts from the "signs" we see to the God we don't see and we believe that He alone is our only ticket out.

When Joseph saw that the butler was being restored to Pharaoh, he wanted the butler to tell Pharaoh about him. "This is my ticket out of here!" he said to himself. Joseph was hoping Pharaoh would then hear his case, take pity on his plight, and release him from prison. Since there was no way for Joseph to appeal his sentence, he was seeking a pardon from the only "supreme court" in the country—Pharaoh himself.

He poured out his heart with great expectation that his case would come to Pharaoh's attention: "I was stolen away! I was falsely accused! Everything that is happening to me shouldn't be happening to me! I am so hurt, so broken."

Wow, I am certain this sounds just like some of us, especially when we don't understand the providence of God. Isn't it amazing how God can conceal destiny in what you think is a disaster? Remember that God is in control of all things at all times and that He is your only ticket out.

Joseph felt for certain the butler was his ticket out of prison. But, to his surprise, God was not ready to let him out. Joseph tried to help God by telling the butler his tragic story and asking the butler to mention him to the one person who could change his circumstance. I believe Joseph even started crying as he related his ordeal so he would make an impression on the butler. That would make it easier for the butler to remember him when he was back in Pharaoh's presence.

But what happened? The chief butler returned to Pharaoh's service and forgot all about Joseph! Your crying won't change God's timing.

Joseph was trying to give God a hand with his release—like so many of us have attempted to do. He sent a message, so to speak, to Pharaoh, but God made sure the message wasn't delivered! As you read this book, I want to encourage you to stay out of God's way because He knows exactly what He is doing. He has in mind the date and the time for you to shine. The Bible promises us that God makes everything beautiful in His time:

> He has made everything beautiful in its appropriate time.
> —ECCLESIASTES 3:11

Yes, God intended to release Joseph from prison. But He was going to do it His way and in His time. God was in control of Joseph's destiny, just as He is in control of your destiny. He alone would get the glory at the end of the day. *So remember, God is your only ticket out!*

Your Current Situation Is Not Your Final Destination

Joseph's current situation was prison, but his final destination was the palace. It's not your now but your latter that God has ordained to be greater. Joseph knew Pharaoh's butler. He was "networked" into Pharaoh's circle. But having a connection with the butler didn't matter—until God's timing had been fulfilled. When it was, then his connection with the butler became very strategic. Ultimately, it doesn't matter who you know unless God deems those relationships as important to His plan for you.

It doesn't matter who you know or who you ask or where you go for help, you cannot interrupt God's timing for your life.

I love it when God is all about being God. I love that He loves us so much He will disrupt our plans in order to fulfill His! Things you know should come easy, that should take care of your problems, don't. Someone you know who has the answer suddenly cannot help you. Why? Because it's not time yet for your change; God isn't finished yet. And He loves you enough that He doesn't want you to come out of your ordeal prematurely and miss your season of development. Here is what the Bible says:

> Unless a grain of wheat falls into the ground and dies, it remains alone. But if it dies, it bears much fruit.
> —JOHN 12:24

God wants us to stop fighting and let Him navigate us to our destiny. So stop fighting, your current situation is not your final destination; stop meddling with the process so that you can receive the promise. You were born to reign!

So, we saw that the butler forgot Joseph. If the butler had remembered him and told Pharaoh about him, then he might have gotten Joseph released. If he had, Joseph would have missed the absolute most important step in his destiny. Missing it would have meant he also would have missed the purpose God had been preparing him for during his long and tragic ordeal. All the suffering he had endured, the lessons he had learned, the character-building he had gone through, and the faithfulness he had held fast to would have been a waste of time if Joseph had been released before God intended for him to be.

Be still and wait on God's timing.

The fact is, liberty was not coming to Joseph for two more years. Joseph had to stay in prison that long because it came to pass after the end of two full years—in God's perfect timing—that Pharaoh dreamed. Every second, minute, hour, day, and year of your life is totally calculated by God to bring about His perfect will concerning you.

The most powerful ruler in the entire known world was about to have a mysterious and troubling dream for which he had no answers. If Joseph had gotten an early release, then he would have missed his chance to interpret that dream—and you would not be reading this book right now!

> After two whole years, Pharaoh had a dream....In the morning his spirit was troubled, and he sent and called for all the magicians of Egypt and all its wise men. Pharaoh told them his dreams, but there was no one who could interpret them to Pharaoh....So Pharaoh sent and called for Joseph, and they brought him hastily out of the dungeon.
> —Genesis 41:1, 8, 14

God allowed Pharaoh to have two dreams in one night. Both disturbed him, and he woke up the next morning troubled. He was all upset by his dream and had no clue what it meant. His royal magicians were known for their skills, which included the accurate interpretations of dreams. But they couldn't figure this latest one out. None of them even remotely had an answer for their boss. God had made dark and difficult their discernment of Pharaoh's dreams. This one had been personally planned by Him (God). He had reserved the interpretation for one man only—a foreign-born state prisoner who was locked away and forgotten in an Egyptian federal prison. Wow—I told you that what God has for you is for *you!*

God will hasten His word to perform it, according to Jeremiah 1:12: "I will hasten My word to perform it." Some of you reading this are saying: "Pastor, *when*? When is He going to hasten His word?" When His chosen time has come, the same way He did with Joseph.

You might wait for years for something to come to pass, and suddenly you wake up one day and it's "manifestation time!"

That's what Joseph experienced—a *suddenly*. Get ready for your *suddenly*—for the moment when you will go from the prison to the palace.

And, so, God also suddenly caused Pharaoh to dream. And Pharaoh's dream coincided directly with the fulfillment of Joseph's destiny, for it was time to transform the dream God had given Joseph into a reality. While he was in prison, the only person in the natural world who could help Joseph was Pharaoh. So God enacted His plan for Pharaoh to have need of Joseph:

- God created a mystery in the palace that only a prisoner in the dungeon could solve.

- God created a problem at the top with the solution at the bottom.

- The man at the top had a need that only the man at the bottom could meet.

- Joseph's anointing was urgently needed.

- The prison doors flew open and out he came.

- He was called up from the prison to the palace.

When God is ready, you will experience a *suddenly*, and remember, that your current situation is not your final destination.

A Divine Setup

> It is as I have spoken to Pharaoh. God has shown Pharaoh what He is about to do. Seven years of great abundance will come throughout all the land of Egypt. However, there will arise after them seven years of famine. All the abundance will be forgotten in the land of Egypt, and the famine will consume the land. The abundance will be unknown in the land because of the famine following, for it will be very severe. The reason the dream was repeated to Pharaoh twice is because the matter is established by God, and God will soon bring it to pass.
> —Genesis 41:28–32

God showed Pharaoh in his dream what was about to happen in his nation. Yet because Pharaoh did not know what his dream meant or the One who had given it to him, he needed Joseph and therefore had to send for him. *A divine setup it was!*

So Joseph said to Pharaoh, "The dream you've had was

shown to you twice because it was established by God that a grievous famine will hit Egypt. And God has revealed to me what must be done about it."

So the slave counseled the Pharaoh. "You must find a man who is wise, who is discrete and he must gather all the food during the seven years of plenty and store it up for the seven years of famine," he said (see Genesis 41:25-36). Notice Joseph did not recommend himself for the job. He was standing in Pharaoh's presence having just interpreted the king's dream, having just won the stunned ruler's favor and respect. Yet he did not recommend himself as the best candidate for the position—he didn't rush to hand Pharaoh his résumé and tell him why his experience made him the right man for the job, even when doing so may have resulted in his freedom forever from his life in the dungeon.

Why not? Because by now Joseph understood that getting into God's business was too costly. It meant only more time and more delay. He knew it was best to let go and let God. He had learned the fact that when you put God second in your life, you will never have first place experiences. Having reached a place of total humility, Joseph refused to blow his own horn or ring his own bell; Joseph was ready for God's next move. Joseph's prison days had came to an end.

Like Joseph, your process has an expiration date. Noticed that when God's time came for Joseph's elevation, He was willing to interrupt the entire world's economy just to take the one He loved and had chosen to the top! God had declared His intention and nothing was going to stop His word from coming to pass—Joseph was born to reign!

The Palace

GOD MAKES HIS MOVE

> And Pharaoh said to Joseph, "Since God has shown you all this...you will be over my house, and according to your word all my people will be ruled.... See, I have set you over all the land of Egypt."
> —GENESIS 41:39–41

Pharaoh exclaimed to his officials and servants: "Can we find such a one as *this man*, a man in whom the Spirit of God is? Can we find anyone who is wiser than this prisoner anointed by God Himself?" Amazing!

What brought Joseph out of the prison was the same thing that had spared his life in the pit, that had elevated him in both Potiphar's house and the prison, and that now had given him the undivided attention and respect of Pharaoh himself. It was the favor of God. God had spoken a word over His favored servant, and God's word does not return to Him void. It accomplishes the purpose for which it is intended:

> So shall My word be that goes forth from My mouth; it shall not return to Me void, but it shall accomplish that which I please, and it shall prosper in the thing for which I sent it.
> —ISAIAH 55:11

How miraculous is this when you think about it—Pharaoh gave a prisoner the keys to the kingdom of Egypt and said to him, "All the people who are under me are now under you." Why would he take a sentenced criminal and put him in charge of not only the royal court but also the entire nation?

That is the power of God, that is the favor of God, that

is the providence of God. When you are born to reign, you may start out in the pit and pass through the prison; but you will eventually be called up to the palace. God had just placed His chosen servant at the very top of the national government. *Just like that. In a moment of time, God makes His move.*

He had planned it that way and He had executed His plan. And in literally a moment in time He had raised up Joseph to the throne. Joseph was elevated to the point that only in the throne would Pharaoh be greater than him.

God had proved His heart and His will to Joseph, just as He will prove His heart and His will to you. To Israel, God's chosen people, He said, "But you must remember the LORD your God, for it is He who gives you the ability to get wealth" (Deut. 8:18). Get ready; for your eye hath not seen nor ear heard what God has prepared (Isa. 64:4), and the only thing God requires of you, is that you remember Him by keeping His laws and commandments.

WHEN YOU ARE DOWN TO NOTHING, GOD IS UP TO SOMETHING

When you are down to nothing, when you don't know what else to do, when you don't even have a preview or the slightest idea that God is working to bring you to the top, just be still and see the salvation of God. He is coming from another angle. Joseph had persistent faith.

Don't let what you are going through blur your vision. If God said it, He will see to it. When times get hard and situations become difficult, remind yourself that in His time He makes everything beautiful (Eccles. 3:11).

The more God desires to favor an individual, the more He invests in building their character. That is what happened to Joseph and what is probably happening to you. Look at Jesus: it took more than thirty years for Him to be prepared for a three-and-a-half year ministry. Joseph had to wait thirteen years—from age seventeen to age thirty—before his dreams became reality.

You may not understand what is going on in your life right now. You may be confused, you may be in a continual fight, you may be troubled, you may be down to nothing; but I guarantee you that God is up to something.

Joseph was in the same position. He did not know that God was building his character so He could take him to the palace. If he believed that at all, it was only by faith. Nothing in the natural had indicated it. He stood by faith and continued to trust God and fear Him. And God came through—big time! Remember, God's ways are not your ways (Isa. 55:8–9).

Get ready because God is preparing you for the greater and like Joseph, you were born to reign!

Chapter Five

BORN TO REIGN!

Born (literal): Brought forth by birth; possessing from birth specified qualities; being in specified circumstances from birth; destined from birth.

Reign (literal): To hold supreme power and dignity in a kingdom or empire; to possess or exercise sovereign power; to govern as king, emperor, or royal ruler.

And Pharaoh said to Joseph…, "You will be over my house, and according to your word all my people will be ruled. Only in regard to the throne will I be greater than you." Then Pharaoh said to Joseph, "See, I have set you over all the land of Egypt." Pharaoh took off his ring from his hand and put it on Joseph's hand and arrayed him in clothes of fine linen and put a gold chain around his neck.
—Genesis 41:39–42

W E CAN SEE from the definition of *born* that we are endued from birth with specific, necessary abilities that pertain to our destiny. What is our destiny?

The specifics differ for each of us, depending on God's purpose in each of our lives. But our ultimate destiny is to rule and reign with Christ:

> [God] made us alive together with Christ (by grace you have been saved), and He raised us up and seated us together in the heavenly places in Christ Jesus.
> —Ephesians 2:5–6

> If we suffer [with Him], we shall also reign with him.
> —2 Timothy 2:12, kjv

We see from the English dictionary that *reign* means to have dominating power or influence—to have control, to govern or rule.

The definition of the word *reign* in both the Hebrew and the Greek includes the dual meaning of ruling *with* authority. We possess that authority because of Christ, because we are in Him and He is in us, and we share in His victory. Yet God will also teach us and test us so that we are wise like Him in the use of that authority.

Rules for Reigning

Just like He did with Joseph, God will process you before He elevates you. He does this because giving power and influence to an immature person is destructive. The key to your success is to stay on the potter's wheel so that He can shape you for your future (see Jeremiah 18:1–6).

God wants us to be brilliant, like a fish in water. Think of the difference between a fish out of water versus one in water. Out of water, a fish flops, flounders, and dies. But in water, it becomes an expression of brilliance—it reflects the wonder of God its Creator as it swims effortlessly and beautifully. A fish that is "in water" lives where it was created to live, doing what it was created to do.

When we are fully prepared for the promise, we too become a reflection of His creative genius. We too are brilliant—because we are in Him. That is where we were created to be:

> Blessed be the God and Father of our Lord Jesus Christ, who has blessed us with every spiritual blessing in the heavenly places in Christ, just as He chose us in Him before the foundation of the world, to be holy and blameless before Him in love.
> —Ephesians 1:3–4

And where we do what we were created to do:

> For we are his workmanship, created in Christ Jesus for good works, which God prepared beforehand, so that we should walk in them.
> —Ephesians 2:10

But in order to actually rule and reign with Him, you too, like Joseph, must be in the right place, doing what you were called to do. Allowing God to prepare us, or "process" us, puts us in that place.

Adam, before he sinned and his mind was spiritually darkened, lived continuously in the presence of God. Because he did, he was a genius. He was able at first sight to give names to thousands of animals and countless other natural creations he had never seen. The Bible says God simply paraded the animals before Adam to see what He would name them:

> Out of the ground the LORD God formed every beast of the field and every bird of the sky, and brought them to the man to see what he would call them. Whatever the man called every living creature, that was its name.
> —GENESIS 2:19

Adam didn't have to first form a committee, hire a consultant, stage a focus group, or take a survey before He could respond to the task God was giving Him. Nor did he consult a dictionary or a thesaurus or an encyclopedia for ideas. When you are born to reign, God endows you with everything you need. God was pleased to give Adam that authority, and he wielded it wisely and properly before the Lord.

Nothing great or of true value comes into existence overnight. Refinement takes time.

That's why God calls us into a "process," a time of preparation, before we inherit what He has promised us. That's why Joseph had to endure the pit, the party, and the prison before he enjoyed the palace—which was the place where God meant for him to go all along. It was the God-ordained place where he was to reign. So take courage! *The difficult things you are going through are just the vehicles God is using to transport you to your destiny!* Therefore the Bible tells us not to be surprised by God's testings:

> Beloved, do not be surprised at the fiery ordeal that is taking place among you to test you, as though some strange thing happened to you. But rejoice insofar as you share in Christ's sufferings, so that you may rejoice and be glad also in the revelation of His glory.
> —1 PETER 4:12–13

The refining process is no different for us than it was for Joseph. Only the details differ. Joseph's story is not your story or mine. Joseph is only our *model*, our example. By giving us this story of Joseph's life, God is showing us how He scripts our destinies in Him:

> Now all these things happened to them for examples. They are written as an admonition to us.
> —1 Corinthians 10:11

There are two key phases of the process that God takes us through: delay and deliverance. Both are providential (divine, heaven sent, miraculous). Both are accomplished according to His timing and His will. Let's look at "providential delays" first.

Providential Delay

A "providential" delay (holdup, postponement) is a *divine* delay. Joseph was a dreamer and dreamed two mighty dreams, both given by God. About the time he was expecting them to come to pass, he found himself in the pit instead and then in the prison. He didn't realize there would be such a delay in the fulfillment of his dreams. He didn't know he had to be prepared for thirteen years before he could receive the promise. He was being delayed by the Divine.

Providential delays are never easy. But they are designed to focus our faith and increase our dependence on God. God is totally capable of making promises to us and fulfilling them right away. But if He would fulfill them at the moment He speaks them to us, we could not handle them. We would lose them. His promises are way bigger than our capacity to successfully hold on to them when we aren't ready for them. Providential delays are for our benefit.

The Lord delayed Joseph from reigning over his brothers by letting him experience the pit, the party, and the prison. Joseph was cast into prison (though he never broke the law). There is purpose in your pain. It was a providential delay.

When God is ordering your steps, some of what you are going to experience will be things you didn't expect—things that just aren't fair; the type of things you did not bring on yourself. But because of destiny you will go through them.

Think again of Joseph, who—though innocent of any crime—was cast into prison because God was training him to reign. He wound up in prison because he *honored* God! That isn't *fair*—but it wasn't meant to be. It was *providential.*

When you are in the middle of a test like that, it won't make sense to your natural mind. You will think: "I honored God; but why this? Now I'm losing what I thought I had gained. Everything is falling apart." Or, like Joseph may have said: "I honored God with all my heart. Now I'm in prison! *Why?*" (Remember, the Bible never says that any of the trials Joseph went through made sense to him at the time.)

Events like those don't make sense to our natural minds. But at the end they will birth purpose and power.

What to do during a providential delay

When you are in a providential delay, how can you stay in faith, reassured that God is taking you somewhere great?

1. *Keep doing what you're doing.* Don't slack off, even

when you are doing everything possible to be right in the eyes of God yet it seems like the whirlwind is trying to destroy you. Those winds are beating against your house and the rains are drenching you because God is preparing you—He's equipping you for the takeover. He's training you to reign. Joseph's priorities were in place, but look how he was tested. Even while he was enduring what he was going through, he remained faithful.

2. *Keep your eyes on the prize.* Fix your inner gaze straight ahead. Stay focused and remain faithful. It's sad but true: only you can stop the work of the Lord in your life. Your worst haters and your worst enemies joined together don't have what it takes to stop what God has ordained in you. Their defeat is as certain as God's victor, so keep your eyes on the prize!

When you can pursue God even when you can't fully see Him; when you can continue moving in the direction He is taking you in spite of the pain; when you are consistent and persistent to say, "I will not let anything hinder me or stop me from pleasing God," then regardless of all your circumstances, you are on your way to greatness. *Remember, you are experiencing providential delays that are setting you up for your future.*

Providential Deliverance

After providential delay comes providential deliverance (release, rescue). That's when God says "enough is enough!" He sends the "breaker anointing" that smashes every prison bar that held you captive. What has you bound doesn't matter; when it's your time to shine, God will make it happen, just like He did for Joseph. Some of you have almost forgotten what life outside a prison cell—outside of a struggle—looks and feels like; but get ready for a jail break because you were born to reign!

You may not be literally in a *state prison*—but your life is in a *prison state*. God Himself will deliver you. When He comes, you *will* be liberated. Death, hell, and the grave imprisoned Jesus but couldn't keep Him bound. They all lost! Jesus smashed every one of those iron bars and came out covered with all power. Jesus is now *your* deliverer. So say it and believe it: "I'm coming out of this prison, in Jesus's name!"

The spiritual forecast for your life calls for rain: showers of blessings! Joseph was thrown in a pit, his brothers held a party, and afterward he went to prison; yet in the end God rained blessings on him. When God determines to favor you, there is absolutely no one who can overturn His decision.

Providential delay and deliverance belong to God. The timing of it belongs to God alone. And, believe me; God is all about "timing." So, like Joseph, *your time will come!*

Lifted Up!

We saw that while Joseph was in prison, he interpreted the dreams of the baker and the butler. He gave both of them interpretations that were accurate and precise and came true.

Then—suddenly—God's perfect timing arrived. Pharaoh had a dream. And like the baker and butler, he could not understand it, he was troubled by it, and he urgently needed an interpreter:

> After two whole years, Pharaoh had a dream....In the morning his spirit was troubled, and he sent and called for all the magicians of Egypt and all its wise

men. Pharaoh told them his dreams, but there was no one who could interpret them to Pharaoh.
—Genesis 41:1, 8

Pharaoh was given by God a dream that revealed a period of famine was coming in Egypt. There would be seven years of plenty followed by seven years of famine, but the years of famine would be so severe that no one would be able to even recognize that there had been seven years of plenty. But he could not understand his dream. God hid it from him so he would have to call upon Joseph for help.

The butler, upon hearing Pharaoh's anguish, finally told him about Joseph—that while he was in prison he had dreamed and Joseph had interpreted his dream and all Joseph had said came to pass. So Pharaoh summoned Joseph:

> So Pharaoh sent and called for Joseph, and they brought him hastily out of the dungeon.... Pharaoh said to Joseph, "I have dreamed a dream, and there is no one who can interpret it. I have heard it said of you that you can understand a dream to interpret it." Joseph answered Pharaoh, saying, "It is not in me. God will give Pharaoh a favorable answer."
> —Genesis 41:14–16

After Pharaoh relayed his dream, Joseph gave him the interpretation:

> Then Joseph said to Pharaoh, "The dreams of Pharaoh are *one and the same*. God has shown Pharaoh what He is about to do. The seven good cows are seven years, and the seven good ears are seven years. The dreams are one. The seven gaunt

and ugly cows that came up after them are seven years, and the seven empty ears scorched by the east wind will be seven years of famine. It is as I have spoken to Pharaoh. God has shown Pharaoh what He is about to do. Seven years of great abundance will come throughout all the land of Egypt. However, there will arise after them seven years of famine. All the abundance will be forgotten in the land of Egypt, and the famine will consume the land. The abundance will be unknown in the land because of the famine following, for it will be very severe. The reason the dream was repeated to Pharaoh twice is because the matter is established by God, and God will soon bring it to pass."
—Genesis 41:25–32

Then Pharaoh said to Joseph:

And Pharaoh said to Joseph, "Since God has shown you all this, there is no one as discerning and wise as you. You will be over my house, and according to your word all my people will be ruled. Only in regard to the throne will I be greater than you." Then Pharaoh said to Joseph, "See, I have set you over all the land of Egypt."
—Genesis 41:39–41, kjv

Once rejected and despised, held captive in a pit, sold into slavery, and imprisoned on false charges, Joseph is now standing before the greatest ruler in the world being told he will co-rule with him over the entire nation. He will rule over Potiphar, he will rule over Potiphar's wife, he will rule over the prison warden, he will rule over the chief butler. He now rules over every single person in Egypt except Pharaoh himself! The only person he answers to is Pharaoh. He entered Pharaoh's presence that day as a prisoner, a foreigner and an inmate in Egyptian society. He exited Pharaoh's presence as literally second in command over the most powerful, wealthy, intellectual nation in the world.

If that isn't being "lifted up" I don't know what is!

Only a great God can do that. Only a great and mighty God—who is sovereign—can bring a slave into a foreign country and raise him up to be in charge over the entire nation. God is awesome in power. Born to reign!

The ring, the robe, and the necklace

Pharaoh then did three things immediately for Joseph. Each was an official act. Taken together, they signified Joseph's new position in the government and installed him as Pharaoh's right-hand man.

1. *He gave Joseph a ring.* With Pharaoh's ring, Joseph was given authority to sign anything in Pharaoh's stead. When you are born to reign, God is going to give you the influence you need to get things done for the kingdom.

2. *He gave Joseph a robe.* A new robe for Joseph! His previous two coats—the coat of many colors and the servant's coat he wore in Potiphar's house—each had symbolized his "covering," his mantle of authority at that time. They simply were foreshadowing what Joseph's future would look like. Notice he lost both coats, and each time he lost one it was because someone was trying to destroy his future. My friend, your attacks come because of your future.

Remember, your process is part of your promise. Joseph had to lose his first two coats because God was ready to give him a royal robe. If you hold on to the old you'll never experience the new.

Notice that this time Joseph's coat was replaced with a *royal* robe—the gift of a supreme leader, literally and figuratively. Literally, it had been bestowed upon him by the supreme ruler of Egypt. Figuratively, however, it has been bestowed upon him by the Supreme Ruler of the universe, almighty God Himself. Therefore, this robe would never be stripped from him, for it was the covering God Himself had provided for Joseph and sovereignly given to him; and no man was going to take this one away. When you're born to reign, God Himself will robe you.

3. *He gave Joseph a gold necklace.* This too symbolized Pharaoh's authority and represented Joseph's rank. The necklace revealed quickly to everyone who saw him that this man was to be highly revered and respected. Joseph was now fully adorned with the very authority of Pharaoh himself. He was identified as Pharaoh's ruler over the land. He was easily recognizable to everyone as the man in charge. Wow, born to reign!

Shame to Fame

On that day, God showcased Joseph to the entire royal court of Pharaoh. He made known to everyone His man, His servant, His vessel of honor. He displayed His glory to all the amazed Egyptians in attendance. He made it known that every person who had mistreated Joseph along the way now would have to come before him for their deliverance. Truly God is an awesome God!

> Joseph was thirty years old when he stood before Pharaoh, the king of Egypt. And Joseph went out from the presence of Pharaoh and went throughout all the land of Egypt. In the seven abundant years the earth brought forth plentifully. So he gathered up

> all the food of the seven years which was in the land of Egypt and laid up the food in the cities.... Joseph gathered great quantities of grain as the sand of the sea until he stopped measuring it, for it was beyond measure. Before the years of famine came, two sons were born to Joseph, whom Asenath, the daughter of Potiphera priest of On, bore to him. Joseph called the name of the firstborn Manasseh, "For God," he said, "has made me forget all my trouble and all my father's house." The name of the second he called Ephraim, *saying,* "For God has caused me to be fruitful in the land of my affliction."
> —GENESIS 41:46–52

While Joseph was undertaking his first project of storing for the famine, God gave him two sons, Manasseh and Ephraim. Joseph named his first son Manasseh, which in Hebrew means "causing to forget."[1] He gave his son that name because God had caused him to forget the pain of his purpose. Now, that's healing! It is so important to God by the time He elevates you that you forget your pain and focus on your purpose. God does not want bitter folks sitting at the top.

His second son he named Ephraim, which means in Hebrew "fruitful,"[2] because God made him fruitful in the land of his affliction. God is excited about you giving birth in the place where they declared you barren. *I must remind you that your pain has a purpose and that in the fullness of time God will shift you from shame to fame!*

God will never usher you straight to the front row; He will seat you at the back and progressively move you to the front. You too will forget what you went through—because something greater is coming upon you. You've heard the saying, "No pain; no gain." Well, purpose says, "No pain, no reign."

> At that time I will deal with all who oppress you; I will save the lame and gather the outcast; I will give them praise and fame in every land where they have been put to shame.
> —Zephaniah 3:19

Joseph honored God; therefore, God made him fruitful. Where Joseph once endured shame, God gave him fame. He will give you praise and fame right where you were put to shame. And God made sure that the same people, the Egyptians who had wronged him, were present when He did it for him! And He was about to do it in full view of Joseph's brothers.

Prisoner to Prince

> Now when Jacob saw that there was corn in Egypt, Jacob said unto his sons, Why do ye look one upon another? And he said, Behold, I have heard that there is corn in Egypt: get you down thither, and buy for us from thence; that we may live, and not die. And Joseph's ten brethren went down to buy corn in Egypt.
> —Genesis 42:1–3, kjv

Corn in Egypt? Now, I would have expected that the corn would have been in Canaan, but it was in Egypt. Anyone in Canaan who needed grain was going to have to go down to Egypt to get it. God had created a situation in nature that would require the same brothers who threw Joseph into the pit to go into Egypt and bow to him, just as his dream had prophesied they would. A famine arose that hit most of that region of the world, including Canaan. The same ten siblings now were on their way to Egypt—and guess who they were going to meet in charge? Joseph, of course. They had no idea who they were coming to for help. God had orchestrated a divine setup.

The Bible says that Joseph's brothers came and bowed to him. Joseph's first dream was fulfilled right then and there:

> And the sons of Israel came to buy corn among those that came: for the famine was in the land of Canaan. And Joseph was the governor over the land, and he it was that sold to all the people of the land: and Joseph's brethren came, and bowed down themselves before him with their faces to the earth.
> —GENESIS 42:5–6, KJV

But they did not recognize their brother! "Joseph knew his brothers, but they did not know him" (Gen. 42:8). He had been so changed that they could look him right in the face and not know it was him. He had gone from a prisoner to a prince!

JOSEPH THE JUDGE

> Joseph also remembered the dreams that he had dreamed of them. He said to them, "You are spies! You came to see the nakedness of the land!" They said to him, "No, my lord, your servants have come only to buy food."...But he said to them, "No, you have come to see the nakedness of the land!"...He put them all together in custody for three days.
> —GENESIS 42:9–10, 12, 17

Joseph said: "I've got you now!" Joseph accused them all of being spies, knowing it was his opportunity to pay them back for what they had done to him. He threw them for three days into the same prison he had been in!

But I believe Joseph began to think about what God had in store for him. I believe he thought back on all God had done for him, and decided: "I am not going to destroy my future by dealing with my past. It was the past that drove me to my future."

Don't jeopardize your future. Be like Joseph, who had the power in his hand to destroy his brothers but remembered that his pain was ordained. Born to reign!

Joseph the Reconciler

> When Joseph came home, they brought into the house to him the present that they had with them and bowed themselves to him to the ground. He asked them about their well-being and said, "Is your father well, the old man of whom you spoke? Is he still alive?" And they answered, "Your servant our father is in good health. He is still alive." And they bowed down their heads and prostrated themselves. He lifted up his eyes and saw his brother Benjamin, his mother's son, and said, "Is this your younger brother of whom you spoke to me?" And he said, "God be gracious to you, my son."
> —Genesis 43:26–29

Joseph then asked his brothers to tell him about their father (his father) and spoke to their youngest brother, Benjamin (his little brother). Joseph brought all his kindred into his house after a while, after first toying with them, causing them to feel some of the fear and anguish he had felt when he was falsely accused and faced judgment and separation from his family.

The same person who was despised, rejected, and mistreated by his siblings now directed their every move and action in his country. The same person they had left to die God had taken to the top, from slavery to royalty.

Eventually, he revealed himself to them:

> Then Joseph could not restrain himself before all who stood by him, and he cried out, "Make every man go out from me." So no man stood with him when Joseph made himself known to his brothers. He wept so loudly that the Egyptians and the house of Pharaoh heard about it.
> —Genesis 45:1–2

After he reconciled with his brothers, he placed them in his house and fed them. He gave them the best of Egypt to eat and wear and then sent them to Canaan to tell Jacob he was alive. He commanded them to bring Jacob and all their families to Egypt and to live there in Goshen in peace and safety where the famine would not touch them.

Across the land, all the Egyptians had to come to Joseph for food. Apart from him they could not eat. The famine was so severe, only he controlled the food supply—what had been stored up during the seven years of plenty. If the people ran out of money, they brought their cattle. If they ran out of cattle, they appealed to Joseph, "We have nothing else—we can give you ourselves and our land." In other words, Joseph was the man in charge!

To Egyptians, and even the people beyond Egypt, he *was* Pharaoh. Because anyone who needed a meal or had an appeal went to Joseph. Pharaoh had turned everything in his power, except the throne itself, over to him.

How amazing God is!

Joseph was a Hebrew in a strange land, yet God put him in command. He wasn't even Egyptian; he was a stranger in a strange land. There is nothing that God can't do! Joseph had survived the process. He had endured until the end. And look how God honored him. God used him to bring healing to His people. Born to reign!

Time to Reign

It is important that you survive the process too. The devil always attacks you when you're heading somewhere in God. He's after your future. He wants to stop you from *getting and sitting*—from getting to the top and sitting on the throne that God has ordained for you. You can't get to the top if you lose at the bottom, so keep fighting.

You must stay connected to God regardless of how you feel, regardless of what you are going through. Don't ever disconnect from God; you are too close to your promise. God is maturing you just as He did Joseph. He wants you to get to the point that it doesn't matter what comes your way; you will remain constant. To endure to the end and make it to the top you must first master the bottom. *You must learn how to handle the pressure and pain of life while yet giving God the glory no matter what situation or circumstance you encounter.*

He is going to test you before He will bless you, just as He did with Joseph. He has a purpose and plans for your life, so get bold and declare, "No weapon formed against me is going to prosper!" (See Isaiah 54:17.) My friend, when it's your time, it's your time! You were born to reign!

When God's time comes for your life, you will experience a "suddenly" moment. That's when everything comes together. That's when things suddenly turn in your favor. One day you will wake up and you'll ask: "How did this thing happen? The folks who rejected me now respect me. Folks that hated me now favor me. Things I did not have, I now have in abundance."

God is getting ready to change your attire like He did Joseph's. When your time comes, God will command an alignment of everything that completes His will for your life. When your date to be great comes, God will cause everything in your life that has been contrary to His promises concerning you to line up and come into order. *Remember, after preparation comes graduation.* You were born to reign!

God is about to make you say, "*Wow!*" When you see what God has for you, you are going to scream. God is going to blow your mind. Joseph's mind must have been confused during his process, but I guarantee you it was settled when he received the promise. God is about to settle your mind!

Joseph experienced the net and endured the affliction. The Egyptians rode over his head, and he went through fire and through water, but God brought him out into a wealthy place (see Psalm 66:11-12). God will connect you at the appointed time to the right people like He did with Joseph. God connected Joseph to Pharaoh because Pharaoh had what Joseph needed—the ring, the robe, the necklace, the chariot, and the wealth. Joseph went from wearing a prisoner's garment to being adorned with a royal robe. His next stop was the top. My friend, like Joseph, your next stop will be the top. Time to reign!

God will adorn you with a ring, a robe, and a golden necklace. He will spread a table before you in the presence of your enemies. They won't be able to touch you. They won't be able to stop you. Why? Because God has declared: "It is *your* time. The pit is covered. The party is over. The prison is closed. The palace is yours."

What God did for Joseph, He will do for you. Accept His process, believe His promises, and wait for your time. It's your time to be lifted up.

You were born to reign!

NOTES

Chapter One
The Pit

1. *Dictionary.com*, s.v. "envy," http://www.dictionary.com/browse/envy?s=t (accessed May 13, 2016).

2. *Merriam-Webster OnLine*, s.v. "envy," http://www.merriam-webster.com/dictionary/envy (accessed April 21, 2016).

Chapter Five
Born to Reign!

1. Mike Campbell, "Manasseh," *Behind the Name*, http://www.behindthename.com/name/manasseh (accessed April 25, 2016).

2. Mike Campbell, "Ephraim," *Behind the Name*, http://www.behindthename.com/name/ephraim (accessed April 25, 2016).

ABOUT THE AUTHOR

Apostle Dr. Reno I. Johnson is a man guided by the Holy Spirit; he is an ambassador of Christ, he is a Warrior in the faith, an excellent Teacher of God's Word and a Dynamic, Radical Preacher. In addition, he is an author, who has written many books that have broaden the scope of individuals globally and they have helped to usher lost souls into the Kingdom of God. He is married to Shandaly Johnson and has one son and two daughters.

Apostle Johnson was ordained as a Minister at The Voice of Deliverance Disciple Center Ministries, Nassau Bahamas where he served for over thirteen years. By divine appointment today, the call and power of God is being demonstrated in the life of Apostle Johnson in such an awesome way. His unconditional love for people and passion for God's Word has been a transportation that has taken him throughout The World at large preaching the Good News of the Gospel of Jesus Christ.

Most notably, he is the president and Chief Executive Officer (CEO) of Reno I. Johnson Ministries International. He was consecrated to the Office of an Apostle on Sunday, December 5, 2010. He is also the founding pastor of Total Life Church, Orlando, Florida and Divine Encounter Ministries International in Nassau, The Bahamas.

Equally important, he has obtained an Associate Degree from New England Institute of Technology- West Palm Beach, Florida. However, upon receiving the call to ministry Apostle Johnson pursued several Biblical Degrees including a Diploma in Biblical Studies from Liberty

University (Lynchburg, Virginia), an Associate Degree in Biblical Studies, and also an Honorary Doctorate Degree in Theology from Bethel Christian University, At present, he is pursuing higher academia in Theology.

Apostle Johnson is a highly sought after anointed messenger of God, whose passion is to win souls for Christ, and advance the Kingdom of God. 'Touching people, Transforming lives'

CONTACT THE AUTHOR

You can email the author at
renoijohnson@gmail.com or rijmintl@gmail.com

Please visit the author's website for current
phone numbers and address.

www.arjm.org

To order any of Apostle Dr. Reno I. Johnson's Ministry
Resources, Please visit our website, write or call us Today!

For Speaking Engagements please call or email us Today.

Connect with us on social media!

Don't forget to visit our Website!

OTHER BOOKS BY THE AUTHOR

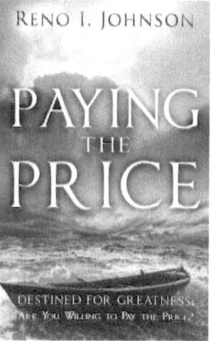

www.ingramcontent.com/pod-product-compliance
Lightning Source LLC
Chambersburg PA
CBHW020657300426
44112CB00007B/425